Two Sunsets & Other Poems by Ella Wheeler Wilcox

Poetry is a fascinating use of language. With almost a million words at its command it is not surprising that these Isles have produced some of the most beautiful, moving and descriptive verse through the centuries. In this series we look at the world through the eyes and minds of our most gifted poets to bring you a unique poetic guide to their lives.

Born on November 5th 1850 in Johnstown, Wisconsin, Ella Wheeler was the youngest of four children. She began to write as a child and by the time she graduated was already well known as a poet throughout Wisconsin.

Regarded more as a popular poet than a literary poet her most famous work 'Solitude' reflects on a train journey she made where giving comfort to a distressed fellow traveller she wrote how the others grief imposed itself for a time on her 'Laugh and the world laughs with you, Weep and you weep alone'. It was published in 1883 and was immensely popular.

The following year, 1884, she married Robert Wilcox. They lived for a time in New York before moving to Connecticut. Their only child, a son, died shortly after birth. It was around this time they developed an interest in spiritualism which for Ella would develop further into an interest in the occult. In later years this and works on positive thinking would occupy much of her writing.

On Robert's death in 1916 she spent months waiting for word from him from 'the other side' which never came.

In 1918 she published her autobiography The Worlds And I.

Ella died of cancer on October 30th, 1919.

Index Of Poems

TWO SUNSETS.

In the fair morning of his life,
When his pure heart lay in his breast,
Panting, with all that wild unrest
To plunge into the great world's strife

That fills young hearts with mad desire,
He saw a sunset. Red and gold
The burning billows surged and rolled,
And upward tossed their caps of fire.

He looked. And as he looked, the sight
Sent from his soul through breast and brain
Such intense joy, it hurt like pain.
His heart seemed bursting with delight.

So near the Unknown seemed, so close
He might have grasped it with his hand.
He felt his inmost soul expand,
As sunlight will expand a rose.

One day he heard a singing strain
A human voice, in bird-like trills.
He paused, and little rapture-rills
Went trickling downward through each vein.

And in his heart the whole day long,
As in a temple veiled and dim,
He kept and bore about with him
The beauty of that singer's song.

And then? But why relate what then?
His smouldering heart flamed into fire
He had his one supreme desire.
And plunged into the world of men.

For years queen Folly held her sway.
With pleasures of the grosser kind
She fed his flesh and drugged his mind,
Till, shamed, he sated turned away.

He sought his boyhood's home. That hour
Triumphant should have been, in sooth,
Since he went forth an unknown youth,
And came back crowned with wealth and power.

The clouds made day a gorgeous bed;
He saw the splendor of the sky
With unmoved heart and stolid eye;
He only knew the West was red.

Then suddenly a fresh young voice

Rose, bird-like, from some hidden place,
He did not even turn his face;
It struck him simply as a noise.

He trod the old paths up and down.
Their rich-hued leaves by Fall winds whirled
How dull they were, how dull the world
Dull even in the pulsing town.

O! worst of punishments, that brings
A blunting of all finer sense,
A loss of feelings keen, intense,
And dulls us to the higher things.

O! penalty most dire, most sure,
Swift following after gross delights,
That we no more see beauteous sights,
Or hear as hear the good and pure.

O! shape more hideous and more dread
Than Vengeance takes in creed-taught minds,
This certain doom that blunts and blinds,
And strikes the holiest feelings dead.

UNREST

In the youth of the year, when the birds were building,
When the green was showing on tree and hedge,
And the tenderest light of all lights was gilding
The world from zenith to outermost edge,
My soul grew sad and longingly lonely!
I sighed for the season of sun and rose,
And I said, "In the Summer and that time only
Lies sweet contentment and blest repose."

With bee and bird for her maids of honor
Came Princess Summer in robes of green.
And the King of day smiled down upon her
And wooed her, and won her, and made her queen.
Fruit of their union and true love's pledges,
Beautiful roses bloomed day by day,
And rambled in gardens and hid in hedges
Like royal children in sportive play.

My restless soul for a little season
Reveled in rapture of glow and bloom,
And then, like a subject who harbors treason,

Grew full of rebellion and gray with gloom.
And I said, "I am sick of the Summer's blisses,
Of warmth and beauty, and nothing more.
The full fruition my sad soul misses
That beauteous Fall time holds in store!"

But now when the colors are almost blinding,
Burning and blending on bush and tree,
And the rarest fruits are mine for the finding,
And the year is ripe as a year can be,
My soul complains in the same old fashion;
Crying aloud in my troubled breast
Is the same old longing, the same old passion.
O where is the treasure which men call rest?

"ARTIST'S LIFE"
Of all the waltzes the great Strauss wrote,
Mad with melody, rhythm rife
From the very first to the final note,
Give me his "Artist's Life!"

It stirs my blood to my finger ends,
Thrills me and fills me with vague unrest,
And all that is sweetest and saddest blends
Together within my breast.

It brings back that night in the dim arcade,
In love's sweet morning and life's best prime.
When the great brass orchestra played and played.
And set our thoughts to rhyme.

It brings back that Winter of mad delights,
Of leaping pulses and tripping feet,
And those languid moon-washed Summer nights
When we heard the band in the street.

It brings back rapture and glee and glow,
It brings back passion and pain and strife,
And so of all the waltzes I know,
Give me the "Artist's Life."

For it is so full of the dear old time
So full of the dear old friends I knew.
And under its rhythm, and lilt, and rhyme,
I am always finding you.

NOTHING BUT STONES

I think I never passed so sad an hour,
Dear friend, as that one at the church to-night.
The edifice from basement to the tower
Was one resplendent blaze of colored light.
Up through broad aisles the stylish crowd was thronging,
Each richly robed like some king's bidden guest.
"Here will I bring my sorrow and my longing,"
I said, "and here find rest."

I heard the heavenly organ's voice of thunder,
It seemed to give me infinite relief.
I wept. Strange eyes looked on in well-bred wonder.
I dried my tears: their gaze profaned my grief.
Wrapt in the costly furs, and silks and laces
Beat alien hearts, that had no part with me.
I could not read, in all those proud cold faces,
One thought of sympathy.

I watched them bowing and devoutly kneeling,
Heard their responses like sweet waters roll.
But only the glorious organ's sacred pealing
Seemed gushing from a full and fervent soul.
I listened to the man of holy calling,
He spoke of creeds, and hailed his own as best;
Of man's corruption and of Adam's falling,
But naught that gave me rest.

Nothing that helped me bear the daily grinding
Of soul with body, heart with heated brain.
Nothing to show the purpose of this blinding
And sometimes overwhelming sense of pain.
And then, dear friend, I thought of thee, so lowly,
So unassuming, and so gently kind,
And lo! a peace, a calm serene and holy,
Settled upon my mind.

Ah, friend, my friend! one true heart, fond and tender,
That understands our troubles and our needs,
Brings us more near to God than all the splendor
And pomp of seeming worship and vain creeds.
One glance of thy dear eyes so full of feeling,
Doth bring me closer to the Infinite,
Than all that throng of worldly people kneeling
In blaze of gorgeous light.

THE COQUETTE

Alone she sat with her accusing heart,
That, like a restless comrade frightened sleep,
And every thought that found her, left a dart
That hurt her so, she could not even weep.

Her heart that once had been a cup well filled
With love's red wine, save for some drops of gall
She knew was empty; though it had not spilled
Its sweets for one, but wasted them on all.

She stood upon the grave of her dead truth,
And saw her soul's bright armor red with rust,
And knew that all the riches of her youth
Were Dead Sea apples, crumbling into dust.

Love that had turned to bitter, biting scorn,
Hearthstones despoiled, and homes made desolate,
Made her cry out that she was ever born,
To loathe her beauty and to curse her fate.

INEVITABLE

To-day I was so weary and I lay
In that delicious state of semi-waking,
When baby, sitting with his nurse at play,
Cried loud for "mamma," all his toys forsaking.

I was so weary and I needed rest,
And signed to nurse to bear him from the room.
Then, sudden, rose and caught him to my breast,
And kissed the grieving mouth and cheeks of bloom.

For swift as lightning came the thought to me,
With pulsing heart-throes and a mist of tears,
Of days inevitable, that are to be,
If my fair darling grows to manhood's years;

Days when he will not call for "mamma," when
The world with many a pleasure and bright joy,
Shall tempt him forth into the haunts of men
And I shall lose the first place with my boy;

When other homes and loves shall give delight,
When younger smiles and voices will seem best.
And so I held him to my heart to-night,

Forgetting all my need of peace and rest.

THE OCEAN OF SONG

In a land beyond sight or conceiving,
In a land where no blight is, no wrong,
No darkness, no graves, and no grieving,
There lies the great ocean of song.
And its waves, oh, its waves unbeholden
By any save gods, and their kind,
Are not blue, are not green, but are golden,
Like moonlight and sunlight combined.

It was whispered to me that their waters
Were made from the gathered-up tears,
That were wept by the sons and the daughters
Of long-vanished eras and spheres.
Like white sands of heaven the spray is
That falls all the happy day long,
And whoever it touches straightway is
Made glad with the spirit of song.

Up, up to the clouds where their hoary
Crowned heads melt away in the skies,
The beautiful mountains of glory
Each side of the song ocean rise.
Here day is one splendor of sky light
Of God's light with beauty replete.
Here night is not night, but is twilight,
Pervading, enfolding and sweet.

Bright birds from all climes and all regions
That sing the whole glad summer long,
Are dumb, till they flock here in legions
And lave in the ocean of song.
It is here that the four winds of heaven,
The winds that do sing and rejoice,
It is here they first came and were given
The secret of sound and a voice.

Far down along beautiful beeches,
By night and by glorious day,
The throng of the gifted ones reaches,
Their foreheads made white with the spray.
And a few of the sons and the daughters
Of this kingdom, cloud-hidden from sight,
Go down in the wonderful waters,

And bathe in those billows of light

And their souls ever more are like fountains,
And liquid and lucent and strong,
High over the tops of the mountains
Gush up the sweet billows of song.
No drouth-time of waters can dry them.
Whoever has bathed in that sea,
All dangers, all deaths, they defy them,
And are gladder than gods are, with glee.

"IT MIGHT HAVE BEEN"
We will be what we could be. Do not say,
"It might have been, had not or that, or this."
No fate can keep us from the chosen way;
He only might, who is.

We will do what we could do. Do not dream
Chance leaves a hero, all uncrowned to grieve.
I hold, all men are greatly what they seem;
He does, who could achieve.

We will climb where we could climb. Tell me not
Of adverse storms that kept thee from the height.
What eagle ever missed the peak he sought?
He always climbs who might.

I do not like the phrase, "It might have been!"
It lacks all force, and life's best truths perverts:
For I believe we have, and reach, and win,
Whatever our deserts.

IF
Dear love, if you and I could sail away,
With snowy pennons to the winds unfurled,
Across the waters of some unknown bay,
And find some island far from all the world;

If we could dwell there, ever more alone,
While unrecorded years slip by apace,
Forgetting and forgotten and unknown
By aught save native song-birds of the place;

If Winter never visited that land,
And Summer's lap spilled o'er with fruits and flowers,

And tropic trees cast shade on every hand,
And twinèd boughs formed sleep-inviting bowers;

If from the fashions of the world set free,
And hid away from all its jealous strife,
I lived alone for you, and you for me
Ah! then, dear love, how sweet were wedded life.

But since we dwell here in the crowded way,
Where hurrying throngs rush by to seek for gold,
And all is common-place and work-a-day,
As soon as love's young honeymoon grows old;

Since fashion rules and nature yields to art,
And life is hurt by daily jar and fret,
'Tis best to shut such dreams down in the heart
And go our ways alone, love, and forget.

GETHSEMANE

In golden youth when seems the earth
A Summer-land of singing mirth,
When souls are glad and hearts are light,
And not a shadow lurks in sight,
We do not know it, but there lies
Somewhere veiled under evening skies
A garden which we all must see
The garden of Gethsemane.

With joyous steps we go our ways,
Love lends a halo to our days;
Light sorrows sail like clouds afar,
We laugh, and say how strong we are.
We hurry on; and hurrying, go
Close to the border-land of woe,
That waits for you, and waits for me
Forever waits Gethsemane.

Down shadowy lanes, across strange streams
Bridged over by our broken dreams;
Behind the misty caps of years,
Beyond the great salt fount of tears,
The garden lies. Strive as you may,
You cannot miss it in your way.
All paths that have been, or shall be,
Pass somewhere through Gethsemane.

All those who journey, soon or late,
Must pass within the garden's gate;
Must kneel alone in darkness there,
And battle with some fierce despair.
God pity those who can not say,
"Not mine but thine," who only pray,
"Let this cup pass," and cannot see
The purpose in Gethsemane.

DUST-SEALED

I know not wherefore, but mine eyes
See bloom, where other eyes see blight.
They find a rainbow, a sunrise,
Where others but discern deep night.

Men call me an enthusiast,
And say I look through gilded haze:
Because where'er my gaze is cast,
I see something that calls for praise.

I say, "Behold those lovely eyes
That tinted cheek of flower-like grace."
They answer in amused surprise:
"We thought it such a common face."

I say, "Was ever scene more fair?
I seem to walk in Eden's bowers."
They answer with a pitying air,
"The weeds are choking out the flowers."

I know not wherefore, but God lent
A deeper vision to my sight.
On whatsoe'er my gaze is bent
I catch the beauty Infinite;

That underlying, hidden half
That all things hold of Deity.
So let the dull crowd sneer and laugh
Their eyes are blind, they cannot see.

"ADVICE"

I must do as you do? Your way I own
Is a very good way. And still,
There are sometimes two straight roads to a town,
One over, one under the hill.

You are treading the safe and the well-worn way,
That the prudent choose each time;
And you think me reckless and rash to-day,
Because I prefer to climb.

Your path is the right one, and so is mine.
We are not like peas in a pod,
Compelled to lie in a certain line,
Or else be scattered abroad.

'Twere a dull old world, methinks, my friend,
If we all went just one way;
Yet our paths will meet no doubt at the end,
Though they lead apart to-day.

You like the shade, and I like the sun;
You like an even pace,
I like to mix with the crowd and run,
And then rest after the race.

I like danger, and storm and strife,
You like a peaceful time;
I like the passion and surge of life,
You like its gentle rhyme.

You like buttercups, dewy sweet,
And crocuses, framed in snow;
I like roses, born of the heat,
And the red carnation's glow.

I must live my life, not yours, my friend,
For so it was written down;
We must follow our given paths to the end,
But I trust we shall meet in town.

OVER THE BANISTERS

Over the banisters bends a face,
Daringly sweet and beguiling.
Somebody stands in careless grace,
And watches the picture, smiling.

The light burns dim in the hall below,
Nobody sees her standing,
Saying good-night again, soft and slow,
Half way up to the landing.

Nobody only the eyes of brown,
Tender and full of meaning,
That smile on the fairest face in town,
Over the banisters leaning.

Tired and sleepy, with drooping head,
I wonder why she lingers;
Now, when the good-nights all are said,
Why somebody holds her fingers.

He holds her fingers and draws her down,
Suddenly growing bolder,
Till the loose hair drops its masses brown
Like a mantle over his shoulder.

Over the banisters soft hands, fair,
Brush his cheeks like a feather,
And bright brown tresses and dusky hair,
Meet and mingle together.

There's a question asked, there's a swift caress,
She has flown like a bird from the hallway,
But over the banisters drops a "yes,"
That shall brighten the world for him alway.

MOMUS, GOD OF LAUGHTER
Though with gods the world is cumbered,
Gods unnamed, and gods unnumbered,
Never god was known to be
Who had not his devotee.
So I dedicate to mine,
Here in verse, my temple-shrine.

'Tis not Ares, mighty Mars,
Who can give success in wars.
'Tis not Morpheus, who doth keep
Guard above us while we sleep,
'Tis not Venus, she whose duty
'Tis to give us love and beauty;
Hail to these, and others, after
Momus, gleesome god of laughter.

Quirinus would guard my health!
Plutus would insure me wealth
Mercury looks after trade,

Hera smiles on youth and maid.
All are kind, I own their worth,
After Momus, god of mirth.

Though Apollo, out of spite,
Hides away his face of light.
Though Minerva looks askance,
Deigning me no smiling glance,
Kings and queens may envy me
While I claim the god of glee.

Wisdom wearies, Love has wings
Wealth makes burdens, Pleasure stings,
Glory proves a thorny crown
So all gifts the gods throw down
Bring their pains and troubles after;
All save Momus, god of laughter.
He alone gives constant joy,
Hail to Momus, happy boy.

I DREAM

Oh, I have dreams. I sometimes dream of Life
In the full meaning of that splendid word.
Its subtle music which few men have heard,
Though all may hear it, sounding through earth's strife.
Its mountain heights by mystic breezes kissed,
Lifting their lovely peaks above the dust;
Its treasures which no touch of time can rust,
Its emerald seas, its dawns of amethyst,
Its certain purpose, its serene repose,
Its usefulness, that finds no hour for woes,
This is my dream of Life.

Yes, I have dreams. I ofttimes dream of Love
As radiant and brilliant as a star.
As changeless, too, as that fixed light afar
Which glorifies vast worlds of space above.
Strong as the tempest when it holds its breath,
Before it bursts in fury; and as deep
As the unfathomed seas, where lost worlds sleep
And sad as birth, and beautiful as death.
As fervent as the fondest soul could crave,
Yet holy as the moonlight on a grave.
This is my dream of Love.

Yes, yes, I dream. One oft-recurring dream,

Is beautiful and comforting and blest.
Complete with certain promises of rest.
Divine content, and ecstasy supreme.
When that strange essence, author of all faith,
That subtle something, which cries for the light,
Like a lost child who wanders in the night,
Shall solve the mighty mystery of Death,
Shall find eternal progress, or sublime
And satisfying slumber for all time.
This is my dream of Death.

THE PAST

I fling my past behind me, like a robe
Worn threadbare in the seams, and out of date.
I have outgrown it. Wherefore should I weep
And dwell upon its beauty, and its dyes
Of Oriental splendor, or complain
That I must needs discard it? I can weave
Upon the shuttles of the future years
A fabric far more durable. Subdued,
It may be, in the blending of its hues,
Where somber shades commingle, yet the gleam
Of golden warp shall shoot it through and through,
While over all a fadeless luster lies,
And starred with gems made out of crystalled tears,
My new robe shall be richer than the old.

THE SONNET

Alone it stands in Poesy's fair land,
A temple by the muses set apart;
A perfect structure of consummate art,
By artists builded and by genius planned.
Beyond the reach of the apprentice hand,
Beyond the ken of the untutored heart,
Like a fine carving in a common mart,
Only the favored few will understand.
A chef-d'oeuvre toiled over with great care,
Yet which the unseeing careless crowd goes by,
A plainly set, but well-cut solitaire,
An ancient bit of pottery, too rare
To please or hold aught save the special eye,
These only with the sonnet can compare.

SECRETS

Think not some knowledge rests with thee alone;
Why, even God's stupendous secret, Death,
We one by one, with our expiring breath,
Do pale with wonder seize and make our own;
The bosomed treasures of the earth are shown,
Despite her careful hiding; and the air
Yields its mysterious marvels in despair
To swell the mighty store-house of things known.
In vain the sea expostulates and raves;
It cannot cover from the keen world's sight
The curious wonders of its coral caves.
And so, despite thy caution or thy tears,
The prying fingers of detective years
Shall drag thy secret out into the light.

A DREAM

That was a curious dream; I thought the three
Great planets that are drawing near the sun
With such unerring certainty, begun
To talk together in a mighty glee.
They spoke of vast convulsions which would be
Throughout the solar system, the rare fun
Of watching haughty stars drop, one by one,
And vanish in a seething vapor sea.

I thought I heard them comment on the earth
That small dark object, doomed beyond a doubt.
They wondered if live creatures moved about
Its tiny surface, deeming it of worth.
And then they laughed, 'twas such a ringing shout
That I awoke and joined too in their mirth.

USELESSNESS

Let mine not be that saddest fate of all
To live beyond my greater self; to see
My faculties decaying, as the tree
Stands stark and helpless while its green leaves fall.
Let me hear rather the imperious call,
Which all men dread, in my glad morning time,
And follow death ere I have reached my prime,
Or drunk the strengthening cordial of life's gall.
The lightning's stroke or the fierce tempest blast
Which fells the green tree to the earth to-day
Is kinder than the calm that lets it last,
Unhappy witness of its own decay.

May no man ever look on me and say,
"She lives, but all her usefulness is past."

WILL

There is no chance, no destiny, no fate,
Can circumvent or hinder or control
The firm resolve of a determined soul.
Gifts count for nothing; will alone is great;
All things give way before it, soon or late.
What obstacle can stay the mighty force
Of the sea-seeking river in its course,
Or cause the ascending orb of day to wait?

Each well-born soul must win what it deserves.
Let the fool prate of luck. The fortunate
Is he whose earnest purpose never swerves,
Whose slightest action or inaction serves
The one great aim.
Why, even Death stands still,
And waits an hour sometimes for such a will.

WINTER RAIN

Falling upon the frozen world last night,
I heard the slow beat of the Winter rain
Poor foolish drops, down-dripping all in vain;
The ice-bound Earth but mocked their puny might,
Far better had the fixedness of white
And uncomplaining snows, which make no sign,
But coldly smile, when pitying moonbeams shine
Concealed its sorrow from all human sight.
Long, long ago, in blurred and burdened years,
I learned the uselessness of uttered woe.
Though sinewy Fate deals her most skillful blow,
I do not waste the gall now of my tears,
But feed my pride upon its bitter, while
I look straight in the world's bold eyes, and smile.

APPLAUSE

I hold it one of the sad certain laws
Which makes our failures sometimes seem more kind
Than that success which brings sure loss behind
True greatness dies, when sounds the world's applause
Fame blights the object it would bless, because
Weighed down with men's expectancy, the mind

Can no more soar to those far heights, and find
That freedom which its inspiration was.
When once we listen to its noisy cheers
Or hear the populace' approval, then
We catch no more the music of the spheres,
Or walk with gods, and angels, but with men.
Till, impotent from our self-conscious fears,
The plaudits of the world turn into sneers.

LIFE

Life, like a romping schoolboy, full of glee,
Doth bear us on his shoulders for a time.
There is no path too steep for him to climb,
With strong, lithe limbs, as agile and as free,
As some young roe, he speeds by vale and sea,
By flowery mead, by mountain peak sublime,
And all the world seems motion set to rhyme,
Till, tired out, he cries, "Now carry me!"
In vain we murmur, "Come," Life says, "fair play!"
And seizes on us. God! he goads us so!
He does not let us sit down all the day.
At each new step we feel the burden grow,
Till our bent backs seem breaking as we go,
Watching for Death to meet us on the way.

BURDENED

"Genius, a man's weapon, a woman's burden." Lamartine.

Dear God! there is no sadder fate in life,
Than to be burdened so that you can not
Sit down contented with the common lot
Of happy mother and devoted wife.

To feel your brain wild and your bosom rife
With all the sea's commotion; to be fraught
With fires and frenzies which you have not sought,
And weighed down with the wide world's weary strife.

To feel a fever alway in your breast,
To lean and hear half in affright, half shame.
A loud-voiced public boldly mouth your name,
To reap your hard-sown harvest in unrest,
And know, however great your meed of fame,
You are but a weak woman at the best.

THE STORY

They met each other in the glade
She lifted up her eyes;
Alack the day! Alack the maid!
She blushed in swift surprise.
Alas! alas! the woe that comes from lifting up the eyes.

The pail was full, the path was steep
He reached to her his hand;
She felt her warm young pulses leap,
But did not understand.
Alas! alas! the woe that comes from clasping hand with hand.

She sat beside him in the wood
He wooed with words and sighs;
Ah! love in spring seems sweet and good,
And maidens are not wise.
Alas! alas! the woe that comes from listing lovers' sighs.

The summer sun shone fairly down,
The wind blew from the south;
As blue eyes gazed in eyes of brown,
His kiss fell on her mouth.
Alas! alas! the woe that comes from kisses on the mouth.

And now the autumn time is near,
The lover roves away,
With breaking heart and falling tear,
She sits the livelong day.
Alas! alas! for breaking hearts when lovers rove away.

LET THEM GO

Let the dream go. Are there not other dreams
In vastness of clouds hid from thy sight
That yet shall gild with beautiful gold gleams,
And shoot the shadows through and through with light?
What matters one lost vision of the night?
Let the dream go!

Let the hope set. Are there not other hopes
That yet shall rise like new stars in thy sky?
Not long a soul in sullen darkness gropes
Before some light is lent it from on high;
What folly to think happiness gone by!
Let the hope set!

Let the joy fade. Are there not other joys,
Like frost-bound bulbs, that yet shall start and bloom?
Severe must be the winter that destroys
The hardy roots locked in their silent tomb.
What cares the earth for her brief time of gloom?
Let the joy fade!

Let the love die. Are there not other loves
As beautiful and full of sweet unrest,
Flying through space like snowy-pinioned doves?
They yet shall come and nestle in thy breast,
And thou shalt say of each, "Lo, this is best!"
Let the love die!

THE ENGINE

Into the gloom of the deep, dark night,
With panting breath and a startled scream;
Swift as a bird in sudden flight
Darts this creature of steel and steam.

Awful dangers are lurking nigh,
Rocks and chasms are near the track,
But straight by the light of its great white eye
It speeds through the shadows, dense and black.

Terrible thoughts and fierce desires
Trouble its mad heart many an hour,
Where burn and smoulder the hidden fires,
Coupled ever with might and power.

It hates, as a wild horse hates the rein,
The narrow track by vale and hill;
And shrieks with a cry of startled pain,
And longs to follow its own wild will.

Oh, what am I but an engine, shod
With muscle and flesh, by the hand of God,
Speeding on through the dense, dark night,
Guided alone by the soul's white light.

Often and often my mad heart tires,
And hates its way with a bitter hate,
And longs to follow its own desires,
And leave the end in the hand of fate.

O mighty engine of steel and steam;
O human engine of blood and bone,
Follow the white light's certain beam
There lies safety and there alone.

The narrow track of fearless truth,
Lit by the soul's great eye of light,
O passionate heart of restless youth,
Alone will carry you through the night.

NOTHING NEW

From the dawn of spring till the year grows hoary,
Nothing is new that is done or said,
The leaves are telling the same old story
"Budding, bursting, dying, dead."
And ever and always the wild bird's chorus
Is "coming, building, flying, fled."

Never the round earth roams or ranges
Out of her circuit, so old, so old,
And the smile o' the sun knows but these changes
Beaming, burning, tender, cold,
As Spring time softens or Winter estranges
The mighty heart of this orb of gold.

From our great sire's birth to the last morn's breaking
There were tempest, sunshine, fruit and frost,
And the sea was calm or the sea was shaking
His mighty main like a lion crossed,
And ever this cry the heart was making
Longing, loving, losing, lost.

Forever the wild wind wanders, crying,
Southerly, easterly, north and west,
And one worn song the fields are sighing,
"Sowing, growing, harvest, rest,"
And the tired thought of the world, replying
Like an echo to what is last and best,
Murmurs "Rest."

DREAMS

Thank God for dreams! I, desolate and lone,
In the dark curtained night, did seem to be
The centre where all golden sun-rays shone,
And, sitting there, held converse sweet with thee.

No shadow lurked between us; all was bright
And beautiful as in the hours gone by,
I smiled, and was rewarded by the light
Of olden days soft beaming from thine eye.
Thank God, thank God for dreams!

I thought the birds all listened; for thy voice
Pulsed through the air, like beat of silver wings.
It made each chamber of my soul rejoice
And thrilled along my heart's tear-rusted strings.
As some devout and ever-prayerful nun
Tells her bright beads, and counts them o'er and o'er,
Thy golden words I gathered, one by one,
And slipped them into memory's precious store.
Thank God, thank God for dreams!

My lips met thine in one ecstatic kiss.
Hand pressed in hand, and heart to heart we sat.
Why even now I am surcharged with bliss
With joy supreme, if I but think of that.
No fear of separation or of change
Crept in to mar our sweet serene content.
In that blest vision, nothing could estrange
Our wedded souls, in perfect union blent.
Thank God, thank God for dreams!

Thank God for dreams! when nothing else is left.
When the sick soul, all tortured wlth Its paln,
Knowing itself forever more bereft,
Finds waiting hopeless and all watching vain,
When empty arms grow rigid with their ache,
When eyes are blinded with sad tides of tears,
When stricken hearts do suffer, yet not break,
For loss of those who come not with the years
Thank God, thank God for dreams!

HELENA

Last night I saw Helena. She whose praise
Of late all men have sounded. She for whom
Young Angus rashly sought a silent tomb
Rather than live without her all his days.

Wise men go mad who look upon her long,
She is so ripe with dangers. Yet meanwhile
I find no fascination in her smile,
Although I make her theme of this poor song.

"Her golden tresses?" yes, they may be fair,
And yet to me each shining silken tress
Seems robbed of beauty and all lustreless
Too many hands have stroked Helena's hair.

(I know a little maiden so demure
She will not let her one true lover's hands
In playful fondness touch her soft brown bands,
So dainty-minded is she, and so pure.)

"Her great dark eyes that flash like gems at night?
Large, long-lashed eyes and lustrous?" that may be,
And yet they are not beautiful to me.
Too many hearts have sunned in their delight.

(I mind me of two tender blue eyes, hid
So underneath white curtains, and so veiled
That I have sometimes plead for hours, and failed
To see more than the shyly lifted lid.)

"Her perfect mouth so like a carvèd kiss?"
"Her honeyed mouth, where hearts do, fly-like, drown?"
I would not taste its sweetness for a crown;
Too many lips have drank its nectared bliss.

(I know a mouth whose virgin dew, undried,
Lies like a young grape's bloom, untouched and sweet,
And though I plead in passion at her feet,
She would not let me brush it if I died.)

In vain, Helena! though wise men may vie
For thy rare smile or die from loss of it,
Armored by my sweet lady's trust, I sit,
And know thou art not worth her faintest sigh.

NOTHING REMAINS
Nothing remains of unrecorded ages
That lie in the silent cemetery of time;
Their wisdom may have shamed our wisest sages,
Their glory may have been indeed sublime.
How weak do seem our strivings after power,
How poor the grandest efforts of our brains,
If out of all we are, in one short hour
Nothing remains.

Nothing remains but the Eternal Spaces,
Time and decay uproot the forest trees.
Even the mighty mountains leave their places,
And sink their haughty heads beneath strange seas;
The great earth writhes in some convulsive spasm
And turns the proudest cities into plains.
The level sea becomes a yawning chasm
Nothing remains.

Nothing remains but the Eternal Forces,
The sad seas cease complaining and grow dry;
Rivers are drained and altered in their courses,
Great stars pass out and vanish from the sky.
Ideas die and old religions perish,
Our rarest pleasures and our keenest pains
Are swept away with all we hate or cherish
Nothing remains.

Nothing remains but the Eternal Nameless
And all-creative spirit of the Law,
Uncomprehended, comprehensive, blameless,
Invincible, resistless, with no flaw;
So full of love it must create forever,
Destroying that it may create again
Persistent and perfecting in endeavor,
It yet must bring forth angels, after men
This, this remains.

LEAN DOWN

Lean down and lift me higher, Josephine!
From the Eternal Hills hast thou not seen
How I do strive for heights? but lacking wings,
I cannot grasp at once those better things
To which I in my inmost soul aspire.
Lean down and lift me higher.

I grope along, not desolate or sad,
For youth and hope and health all keep me glad;
But too bright sunlight, sometimes, makes us blind,
And I do grope for heights I cannot find.
Oh, thou must know my one supreme desire
Lean down and lift me higher.

Not long ago we trod the self-same way.
Thou knowest how, from day to fleeting day
Our souls were vexed with trifles, and our feet,

Were lured aside to by-paths which seemed sweet,
But only served to hinder and to tire;
Lean down and lift me higher.

Thou hast gone onward to the heights serene,
And left me here, my loved one, Josephine;
I am content to stay until the end,
For life is full of promise; but, my friend,
Canst thou not help me in my best desire
And lean, and lift me higher?

Frail as thou wert, thou hast grown strong and wise,
And quick to understand and sympathize
With all a full soul's needs. It must be so,
Thy year with God hath made thee great I know.
Thou must see how I struggle and aspire
Oh, warm me with a breath of heavenly fire,
And lean, and lift me higher.

COMRADES

I and my Soul are alone to-day,
All in the shining weather;
We were sick of the world, and we put it away,
So we could rejoice together.

Our host, the Sun, in the blue, blue sky
Is mixing a rare, sweet wine,
In the burnished gold of his cup on high,
For me, and this Soul of mine.

We find it a safe and royal drink,
And a cure for every pain;
It helps us to love, and helps us to think,
And strengthens body and brain.

And sitting here, with my Soul alone,
Where the yellow sun-rays fall,
Of all the friends I have ever known
I find it the best of all.

We rarely meet when the World is near,
For the World hath a pleasing art
And brings me so much that is bright and dear
That my Soul it keepeth apart.

But when I grow weary of mirth and glee,

Of glitter, and glow, and splendor,
Like a tried old friend it comes to me,
With a smile that is sad and tender.

And we walk together as two friends may,
And laugh, and drink God's wine.
Oh, a royal comrade any day
I find this Soul of mine.

WHAT GAIN?

Now, while thy rounded cheek is fresh and fair,
While beauty lingers, laughing, in thine eyes,
Ere thy young heart shall meet the stranger, "Care,"
Or thy blithe soul become the home of sighs,
Were it not kindness should I give thee rest
By plunging this sharp dagger in thy breast?
Dying so young, with all thy wealth of youth,
What part of life wouldst thou not claim, in sooth?
Only the woe,
Sweetheart, that sad souls know.

Now, in this sacred hour of supreme trust,
Of pure delight and palpitating joy,
Ere change can come, as come it surely must,
With jarring doubts and discords, to destroy
Our far too perfect peace, I pray thee, Sweet,
Were it not best for both of us, and meet,
If I should bring swift death to seal our bliss?
Dying so full of joy, what could we miss?
Nothing but tears,
Sweetheart, and weary years.

How slight the action! Just one well-aimed blow
Here where I feel thy warm heart's pulsing beat,
And then another through my own, and so
Our perfect union would be made complete:
So past all parting, I should claim thee mine.
Dead with our youth, and faith, and love divine,
Should we not keep the best of life that way?
What shall we gain by living day on day?
What shall we gain,
Sweetheart, but bitter pain?

LIFE

I feel the great immensity of life.

All little aims slip from me, and I reach
My yearning soul toward the Infinite.

As when a mighty forest, whose green leaves
Have shut it in, and made it seem a bower
For lovers' secrets, or for children's sports,
Casts all its clustering foliage to the winds,
And lets the eye behold it, limitless,
And full of winding mysteries of ways:
So now with life that reaches out before,
And borders on the unexplained Beyond.

I see the stars above me, world on world:
I hear the awful language of all Space;
I feel the distant surging of great seas,
That hide the secrets of the Universe
In their eternal bosoms; and I know
That I am but an atom of the Whole.

TO THE WEST

Not to the crowded East,
Where, in a well-worn groove,
Like the harnessed wheel of a great machine,
The trammeled mind must move
Where Thought must follow the fashion of Thought,
Or be counted vulgar and set at naught.

Not to the languid South,
Where the mariners of the brain
Are lured by the Sirens of the Sense,
And wrecked upon its main
Where Thought is rocked, on the sweet wind's breath,
To a torpid sleep that ends in death.

But to the mighty West,
That chosen realm of God,
Where Nature reaches her hands to men,
And Freedom walks abroad
Where mind is King, and fashion is naught:
There shall the New World look for thought.

To the West, the beautiful West,
She shall look, and not in vain
For out of its broad and boundless store
Come muscle, and nerve, and brain.
Let the bards of the East and the South be dumb

For out of the West shall the Poets come.

They shall come with souls as great
As the cradle where they were rocked;
They shall come with brows that are touched with fire,
Like the Gods with whom they have walked;
They shall come from the West in royal state,
The Singers and Thinkers for whom we wait.

THE LAND OF CONTENT

I set out for the Land of Content,
By the gay crowded pleasure-highway,
With laughter, and jesting, I went
With the mirth-loving throng for a day;
Then I knew I had wandered astray,
For I met returned pilgrims, belated,
Who said, "We are weary and sated,
But we found not the Land of Content."

I turned to the steep path of fame,
I said, "It is over yon height
This land with the beautiful name
Ambition will lend me its light."
But I paused in my journey ere night,
For the way grew so lonely and troubled;
I said, my anxiety doubled
"This is not the road to Content."

Then I joined the great rabble and throng
That frequents the moneyed world's mart;
But the greed, and the grasping and wrong,
Left me only one wish to depart.
And sickened, and saddened at heart,
I hurried away from the gateway,
For my soul and my spirit said straightway,
"This is not the road to Content."

Then weary in body and brain,
An overgrown path I detected,
And I said "I will hide with my pain
In this by-way, unused and neglected."
Lo! it led to the realm God selected
To crown with his best gifts of beauty,
And through the dark pathway of duty
I came to the land of Content.

A SONG OF LIFE

In the rapture of life and of living,
I lift up my heart and rejoice,
And I thank the great Giver for giving
The soul of my gladness a voice.
In the glow of the glorious weather,
In the sweet-scented sensuous air,
My burdens seem light as a feather
They are nothing to bear.

In the strength and the glory of power,
In the pride and the pleasure of wealth,
(For who dares dispute me my dower
Of talents and youth-time and health?)
I can laugh at the world and its sages
I am greater than seers who are sad,
For he is most wise in all ages
Who knows how to be glad.

I lift up my eyes to Apollo,
The god of the beautiful days,
And my spirit soars off like a swallow
And is lost in the light of its rays.
Are you troubled and sad? I beseech you
Come out of the shadows of strife
Come out in the sun while I teach you
The secret of life.

Come out of the world, come above it
Up over its crosses and graves,
Though the green earth is fair and I love it,
We must love it as masters, not slaves.
Come up where the dust never rises
But only the perfume of flowers
And your life shall be glad with surprises
Of beautiful hours.
Come up where the rare golden wine is
Apollo distills in my sight,
And your life shall be happy as mine is,
And as full of delight.

WARNING

High in the heavens I saw the moon this morning,
Albeit the sun shone bright;
Unto my soul it spoke, in voice of warning,

"Remember Night!"

THE CHRISTIAN'S NEW YEAR PRAYER

Thou Christ of mine, thy gracious ear low bending
Through these glad New Year days,
To catch the countless prayers to Heaven ascending
For e'en hard hearts do raise
Some secret wish for fame, or gold, or power,
Or freedom from all care
Dear, patient Christ, who listeneth hour on hour,
Hear now a Christian's prayer.

Let this young year that, silent, walks beside me,
Be as a means of grace
To lead me up, no matter what betide me,
Nearer the Master's face.
If it need be that ere I reach the fountain
Where Living waters play,
My feet should bleed from sharp stones on the mountain,
Then cast them in my way.

If my vain soul needs blows and bitter losses
To shape it for thy crown,
Then bruise it, burn it, burden it with crosses,
With sorrows bear it down.
Do what thou wilt to mold me to thy pleasure,
And if I should complain,
Heap full of anguish yet another measure
Until I smile at pain.
Send dangers, deaths! but tell me how to dare them;
Enfold me in thy care.
Send trials, tears! but give me strength to bear them
This is a Christian's prayer.

IN THE NIGHT

Sometimes at night, when I sit and write,
I hear the strangest things,
As my brain grows hot with burning thought,
That struggles for form and wings,
I can hear the beat of my swift blood's feet,
As it speeds with a rush and a whir
From heart to brain and back again,
Like a race-horse under the spur.

With my soul's fine ear I listen and hear

The tender Silence speak,
As it leans on the breast of Night to rest,
And presses his dusky cheek.
And the darkness turns in its sleep, and yearns
For something that is kin;
And I hear the hiss of a scorching kiss,
As it folds and fondles Sin.

In its hurrying race through leagues of space,
I can hear the Earth catch breath,
As it heaves and moans, and shudders and groans,
And longs for the rest of Death.
And high and far, from a distant star,
Whose name is unknown to me,
I hear a voice that says, "Rejoice,
For I keep ward o'er thee!"

Oh, sweet and strange are the sounds that range
Through the chambers of the night;
And the watcher who waits by the dim, dark gates,
May hear, if he lists aright.

GOD'S MEASURE
God measures souls by their capacity
For entertaining his best Angel, Love.
Who loveth most is nearest kin to God,
Who is all Love, or Nothing.
He who sits
And looks out on the palpitating world,
And feels his heart swell in him large enough
To hold all men within it, he is near
His great Creator's standard, though he dwells
Outside the pale of churches, and knows not
A feast-day from a fast-day, or a line
Of Scripture even. What God wants of us
Is that outreaching bigness that ignores
All littleness of aims, or loves, or creeds,
And clasps all Earth and Heaven in its embrace.

A MARCH SNOW
Let the old snow be covered with the new:
The trampled snow, so soiled, and stained, and sodden.
Let it be hidden wholly from our view
By pure white flakes, all trackless and untrodden.
When Winter dies, low at the sweet Spring's feet,

Let him be mantled in a clean, white sheet.

Let the old life be covered by the new:
The old past life so full of sad mistakes,
Let it be wholly hidden from the view
By deeds as white and silent as snow-flakes.
Ere this earth life melts in the eternal Spring
Let the white mantle of repentance, fling
Soft drapery about it, fold on fold,
Even as the new snow covers up the old.

AFTER THE BATTLES ARE OVER

After the battles are over,
And the war drums cease to beat,
And no more is heard on the hillside
The sound of hurrying feet,
Full many a noble action,
That was done in the days of strife,
By the soldier is half forgotten,
In the peaceful walks of life.

Just as the tangled grasses,
In Summer's warmth and light,
Grow over the graves of the fallen
And hide them away from sight,
So many an act of valor,
And many a deed sublime,
Fade from the mind of the soldier,
O'ergrown by the grass of time.

Not so should they be rewarded,
Those noble deeds of old;
They should live forever and ever,
When the heroes' hearts are cold.
Then rally, ye brave old comrades,
Old veterans, re-unite!
Uproot Time's tangled grasses
Live over the march, and the fight.

Let Grant come up from the White House,
And clasp each brother's hand,
First chieftain of the army,
Last chieftain of the land.
Let him rest from a nation's burdens,
And go, in thought, with his men,
Through the fire and smoke of Shiloh,

And save the day again.

This silent hero of battles
Knew no such word as defeat.
It was left for the rebels' learning,
Along with the word retreat.
He was not given to talking,
But he found that guns would preach
In a way that was more convincing
Than fine and flowery speech.

Three cheers for the grave commander
Of the grand old Tennessee!
Who won the first great battle
Gained the first great victory.
His motto was always "Conquer,"
"Success" was his countersign,
And "though it took all Summer,"
He kept fighting upon "that line."

Let Sherman, the stern old General,
Come rallying with his men;
Let them march once more through Georgia
And down to the sea again.
Oh! that grand old tramp to Savannah,
Three hundred miles to the coast,
It will live in the heart of the nation,
Forever its pride and boast.

As Sheridan went to the battle,
When a score of miles away,
He has come to the feast and banquet,
By the iron horse, to-day.
Its pace is not much swifter
Than the pace of that famous steed
Which bore him down to the contest
And saved the day by his speed.

Then go over the ground to-day, boys,
Tread each remembered spot.
It will be a gleesome journey,
On the swift-shod feet of thought;
You can fight a bloodless battle,
You can skirmish along the route,
But it's not worth while to forage,
There are rations enough without.

Don't start if you hear the cannon,
It is not the sound of doom,
It does not call to the contest
To the battle's smoke and gloom.
"Let us have peace," was spoken,
And lo! peace ruled again;
And now the nation is shouting,
Through the cannon's voice, "Amen."

O boys who besieged old Vicksburg,
Can time e'er wash away
The triumph of her surrender,
Nine years ago to-day?
Can you ever forget the moment,
When you saw the flag of white,
That told how the grim old city
Had fallen in her might?

Ah, 'twas a bold brave army,
When the boys, with a right good will,
Went gayly marching and singing
To the fight at Champion Hill.
They met with a warm reception,
But the soul of "Old John Brown"
Was abroad on that field of battle,
And our flag did NOT go down.

Come, heroes of Look Out Mountain,
Of Corinth and Donelson,
Of Kenesaw and Atlanta,
And tell how the day was won!
Hush! bow the head for a moment
There are those who cannot come.
No bugle-call can arouse them
No sound of fife or drum.

Oh, boys who died for the country,
Oh, dear and sainted dead!
What can we say about you
That has not once been said?
Whether you fell in the contest,
Struck down by shot and shell,
Or pined 'neath the hand of sickness
Or starved in the prison cell,

We know that you died for Freedom,
To save our land from shame,

To rescue a periled Nation,
And we give you deathless fame.
'T was the cause of Truth and Justice
That you fought and perished for,
And we say it, oh, so gently,
"Our boys who died in the war."

Saviors of our Republic,
Heroes who wore the blue,
We owe the peace that surrounds us
And our Nation's strength to you.
We owe it to you that our banner,
The fairest flag in the world,
Is to-day unstained, unsullied,
On the Summer air unfurled.

We look on its stripes and spangles,
And our hearts are filled the while
With love for the brave commanders,
And the boys of the rank and file.
The grandest deeds of valor
Were never written out,
The noblest acts of virtue
The world knows nothing about.

And many a private soldier,
Who walks his humble way,
With no sounding name or title,
Unknown to the world to-day,
In the eyes of God is a hero
As worthy of the bays,
As any mighty General
To whom the world gives praise.

Brave men of a mighty army,
We extend you friendship's hand!
I speak for the "Loyal Women,"
Those pillars of our land.
We wish you a hearty welcome,
We are proud that you gather here
To talk of old times together
On this brightest day in the year.

And if Peace, whose snow-white pinions,
Brood over our land to-day,
Should ever again go from us,
(God grant she may ever stay!)

Should our Nation call in her peril
For "Six hundred thousand more,"
The loyal women would hear her,
And send you out as before.

We would bring out the treasured knapsack,
We would take the sword from the wall,
And hushing our own hearts' pleadings,
Hear only the country's call.
For next to our God, is our Nation;
And we cherish the honored name,
Of the bravest of all brave armies
Who fought for that Nation's fame.

NOBLESSE OBLIGE

I hold it the duty of one who is gifted,
And specially dowered in all men's sight,
To know no rest till his life is lifted
Fully up to his great gifts' height.

He must mold the man into rare completeness,
For gems are set only in gold refined.
He must fashion his thoughts into perfect sweetness,
And cast out folly and pride from his mind.

For he who drinks from a god's gold fountain
Of art or music or rhythmic song
Must sift from his soul the chaff of malice,
And weed from his heart the roots of wrong.

Great gifts should be worn, like a crown befitting!
And not like gems in a beggar's hands.
And the toil must be constant and unremitting
Which lifts up the king to the crown's demands.

AND THEY ARE DUMB

I have been across the bridges of the years.
Wet with tears
Were the ties on which I trod, going back
Down the track
To the valley where I left, 'neath skies of Truth,
My lost youth.

As I went, I dropped my burdens, one and all
Let them fall;

All my sorrows, all my wrinkles, all my care,
My white hair,
I laid down, like some lone pilgrim's heavy pack,
By the track.

As I neared the happy valley with light feet,
My heart beat
To the rhythm of a song I used to know
Long ago,
And my spirits gushed and bubbled like a fountain
Down a mountain.

On the border of that valley I found you,
Tried and true;
And we wandered through the golden Summer-Land
Hand in hand.
And my pulses beat with rapture in the blisses
Of your kisses.

And we met there, in those green and verdant places,
Smiling faces,
And sweet laughter echoed upward from the dells
Like gold bells.
And the world was spilling over with the glory
Of Youth's story.

It was but a dreamer's journey of the brain;
And again
I have left the happy valley far behind;
And I find
Time stands waiting with his burdens in a pack
For my back.

As he speeds me, like a rough, well-meaning friend,
To the end,
Will I find again the lost ones loved so well?
Who can tell!
But the dead know what the life will be to come
And they are dumb!

NIGHT

As some dusk mother shields from all alarms
The tired child she gathers to her breast,
The brunette Night doth fold me in her arms,
And hushes me to perfect peace and rest.
Her eyes of stars shine on me, and I hear

Her voice of winds low crooning on my ear.
O Night, O Night, how beautiful thou art!
Come, fold me closer to thy pulsing heart.

The day is full of gladness, and the light
So beautifies the common outer things,
I only see with my external sight,
And only hear the great world's voice which rings
But silently from daylight and from din
The sweet Night draws me, whispers, "Look within!"
And looking, as one wakened from a dream,
I see what is no longer what doth seem.

The Night says, "Listen!" and upon my ear
Revealed, as are the visions to my sight,
The voices known as "Beautiful" come near
And whisper of the vastly Infinite.
Great, blue-eyed Truth, her sister Purity,
Their brother Honor, all converse with me,
And kiss my brow, and say, "Be brave of heart!"
O holy three! how beautiful thou art!

The Night says, "Child, sleep that thou may'st arise
Strong for to-morrow's struggle." And I feel
Her shadowy fingers pressing on my eyes:
Like thistledown I float to the Ideal
The Slumberland, made beautiful and bright
As death, by dreams of loved ones gone from sight,
O food for soul's, sweet dreams of pure delight,
How beautiful the holy hours of Night!

ALL FOR ME
The world grows green on a thousand hills
By a thousand willows the bees are humming,
And a million birds by a million rills,
Sing of the golden season coming.
But, gazing out on the sun-kist lea,
And hearing a thrush and a blue-bird singing,
I feel that the Summer is all for me,
And all for me are the joys it is bringing.

All for me the bumble-bee
Drones his song in the perfect weather;
And, just on purpose to sing to me,
Thrush and blue-bird came North together.
Just for me, in red and white,

Bloom and blossom the fields of clover;
And all for me and my delight
The wild Wind follows and plays the lover.

The mighty sun, with a scorching kiss
(I have read, and heard, and do not doubt it)
Has burned up a thousand worlds like this,
And never stopped to think about it.
And yet I believe he hurries up
Just on purpose to kiss my flowers
To drink the dew from the lily-cup,
And help it to grow through golden hours.

I know I am only a speck of dust,
An individual mite of masses,
Clinging upon the outer crust
Of a little ball of cooling gases.
And yet, and yet, say what you will,
And laugh, if you please, at my lack of reason,
For me wholly, and for me still,
Blooms and blossoms the Summer season.

Nobody else has ever heard
The story the Wind to me discloses;
And none but I and the humming-bird
Can read the hearts of the crimson roses.
Ah, my Summer, my love, my own!
The world grows glad in your smiling weather;
Yet all for me, and me alone,
You and your Court came north together.

PHILOSOPHY

At morn the wise man walked abroad,
Proud with the learning of great fools.
He laughed and said, "There is no God
'Tis force creates, 'tis reason rules."

Meek with the wisdom of great faith,
At night he knelt while angels smiled,
And wept and cried with anguished breath,
"Jehovah, God, save thou my child."

"CARLOS."

Last night I knelt low at my lady's feet.
One soft, caressing hand played with my hair,

And one I kissed and fondled. Kneeling there,
I deemed my meed of happiness complete.

She was so fair, so full of witching wiles
Of fascinating tricks of mouth and eye;
So womanly withal, but not too shy
And all my heaven was compassed by her smiles.

Her soft touch on my cheek and forehead sent,
Like little arrows, thrills of tenderness
Through all my frame. I trembled with excess
Of love, and sighed the sigh of great content.

When any mortal dares to so rejoice,
I think a jealous Heaven, bending low,
Reaches a stern hand forth and deals a blow.
Sweet through the dusk I heard my lady's voice.

"My love!" she sighed, "My Carlos!" even now
I feel the perfumed zephyr of her breath
Bearing to me those words of living death,
And starting out the cold drops on my brow.

For I am Paul not Carlos! Who is he
That, in the supreme hour of love's delight,
Veiled by the shadows of the falling night,
She should breathe low his name, forgetting me?

I will not ask her! 'twere a fruitless task,
For, woman-like, she would make me believe
Some well-told tale; and sigh, and seem to grieve,
And call me cruel. Nay, I will not ask.

But this man Carlos, whosoe'er he be,
Has turned my cup of nectar into gall,
Since I know he has claimed some one or all
Of these delights my lady grants to me.

He must have knelt and kissed her, in some sad
And tender twilight, when the day grew dim.
How else could I remind her so of him?
Why, reveries like these have made men mad!

He must have felt her soft hand on his brow.
If Heaven was shocked at such presumptuous wrongs,
And plunged him in the grave, where he belongs,
Still she remembers, though she loves me now.

And if he lives, and meets me to his cost,
Why, what avails it? I must hear and see
That curst name "Carlos" always haunting me
So has another Paradise been lost.

THE TWO GLASSES

There sat two glasses filled to the brim,
On a rich man's table, rim to rim.
One was ruddy and red as blood,
And one was clear as the crystal flood.

Said the glass of wine to his paler brother,
"Let us tell tales of the past to each other;
I can tell of a banquet, and revel, and mirth,
Where I was king, for I ruled in might;
For the proudest and grandest souls on earth
Fell under my touch, as though struck with blight.
From the heads of kings I have torn the crown;
From the heights of fame I have hurled men down.
I have blasted many an honored name;
I have taken virtue and given shame;
I have tempted the youth with a sip, a taste,
That has made his future a barren waste.
Far greater than any king am I,
Or than any army beneath the sky.
I have made the arm of the driver fail,
And sent the train from the iron rail.
I have made good ships go down at sea,
And the shrieks of the lost were sweet to me.
Fame, strength, wealth, genius before me fall;
And my might and power are over all!
Ho, ho! pale brother," said the wine,
"Can you boast of deeds as great as mine?"

Said the water-glass: "I cannot boast
Of a king dethroned, or a murdered host,
But I can tell of hearts that were sad
By my crystal drops made bright and glad;
Of thirsts I have quenched, and brows I have laved;
Of hands I have cooled, and souls I have saved.
I have leaped through the valley, dashed down the mountain,
Slept in the sunshine, and dripped from the fountain.
I have burst my cloud-fetters, and dropped from the sky.
And everywhere gladdened the prospect and eye;
I have eased the hot forehead of fever and pain;

I have made the parched meadows grow fertile with grain.
I can tell of the powerful wheel of the mill,
That ground out the flour, and turned at my will.
I can tell of manhood debased by you,
That I have uplifted and crowned anew
I cheer, I help, I strengthen and aid;
I gladden the heart of man and maid;
I set the wine-chained captive free,
And all are better for knowing me."

These are the tales they told each other,
The glass of wine and its paler brother,
As they sat together, filled to the brim,
On a rich man's table, rim to rim.

THROUGH TEARS

An artist toiled over his pictures;
He labored by night and by day.
He struggled for glory and honor,
But the world, it had nothing to say.
His walls were ablaze with the splendors
We see in the beautiful skies;
But the world beheld only the colors
That were made out of chemical dyes.

Time sped. And he lived, loved, and suffered;
He passed through the valley of grief.
Again he toiled over his canvas,
Since in labor alone was relief.
It showed not the splendor of colors
Of those of his earlier years,
But the world? the world bowed down before it,
Because it was painted with tears.

A poet was gifted with genius,
And he sang, and he sang all the days.
He wrote for the praise of the people,
But the people accorded no praise.
Oh, his songs were as blithe as the morning,
As sweet as the music of birds;
But the world had no homage to offer,
Because they were nothing but words.

Time sped. And the poet through sorrow
Became like his suffering kind.
Again he toiled over his poems

To lighten the grief of his mind.
They were not so flowing and rhythmic
As those of his earlier years,
But the world? lo! it offered its homage
Because they were written in tears.

So ever the price must be given
By those seeking glory in art;
So ever the world is repaying
The grief-stricken, suffering heart.
The happy must ever be humble;
Ambition must wait for the years,
Ere hoping to win the approval
Of a world that looks on through its tears.

INTO SPACE

If the sad old world should jump a cog
Sometime, in its dizzy spinning,
And go off the track with a sudden jog,
What an end would come to the sinning.
What a rest from strife and the burdens of life
For the millions of people in it,
What a way out of care, and worry and wear,
All in a beautiful minute.

As 'round the sun with a curving sweep
It hurries and runs and races,
Should it lose its balance, and go with a leap
Into the vast sea-spaces,
What a blest relief it would bring to the grief,
And the trouble and toil about us,
To be suddenly hurled from the solar world
And let it go on without us.

With not a sigh or a sad good-by
For loved ones left behind us,
We would go with a lunge and a mighty plunge
Where never a grave should find us.
What a wild mad thrill our veins would fill
As the great earth, life a feather,
Should float through the air to God knows where,
And carry us all together.

No dark, damp tomb and no mourner's gloom,
No tolling bell in the steeple,
But in one swift breath a painless death

For a million billion people.
What greater bliss could we ask than this,
To sweep with a bird's free motion
Through leagues of space to a resting place,
In a vast and vapory ocean
To pass away from this life for aye
With never a dear tie sundered,
And a world on fire for a funeral pyre,
While the stars looked on and wondered?

THROUGH DIM EYES

Is it the world, or my eyes, that are sadder?
I see not the grace that I used to see
In the meadow-brook whose song was so glad, or
In the boughs of the willow tree.
The brook runs slower, its song seems lower,
And not the song that it sang of old;
And the tree I admired looks weary and tired
Of the changeless story of heat and cold.

When the sun goes up, and the stars go under,
In that supreme hour of the breaking day,
Is it my eyes, or the dawn I wonder,
That finds less of the gold, and more of the gray?
I see not the splendor, the tints so tender,
The rose-hued glory I used to see;
And I often borrow a vague half-sorrow
That another morning has dawned for me.

When the royal smile of that welcome comer
Beams on the meadow and burns in the sky,
Is it my eyes, or does the Summer
Bring less of bloom than in days gone by?
The beauty that thrilled me, the rapture that filled me,
To an overflowing of happy tears,
I pass unseeing, my sad eyes being
Dimmed by the shadow of vanished years.

When the heart grows weary, all things seem dreary;
When the burden grows heavy, the way seems long.
Thank God for sending kind death as an ending,
Like a grand Amen to a minor song.

LA MORT D'AMOUR

When was it that love died? We were so fond,

So very fond, a little while ago.
With leaping pulses, and blood all aglow,
We dreamed about a sweeter life beyond,

When we should dwell together as one heart,
And scarce could wait that happy time to come.
Now side by side we sit with lips quite dumb,
And feel ourselves a thousand miles apart.

How was it that love died! I do not know.
I only know that all its grace untold
Has faded into gray! I miss the gold
From our dull skies; but did not see it go.

Why should love die? We prized it, I am sure;
We thought of nothing else when it was ours;
We cherished it in smiling, sunlit bowers;
It was our all; why could it not endure?

Alas, we know not how, or when or why
This dear thing died. We only know it went,
And left us dull, cold, and indifferent;
We who found heaven once in each other's sigh.

How pitiful it is, and yet how true
That half the lovers in the world, one day,
Look questioning in each other's eyes this way
And know love's gone forever, as we do.

Sometimes I cannot help but think, dear heart,
As I look out o'er all the wide, sad earth
And see love's flame gone out on many a hearth,
That those who would keep love must dwell apart.

THE PUNISHED

Not they who know the awful gibbet's anguish,
Not they who, while sad years go by them, in
The sunless cells of lonely prisons languish,
Do suffer fullest penalty for sin.

'Tis they who walk the highways unsuspected
Yet with grim fear forever at their side,
Who hug the corpse of some sin undetected,
A corpse no grave or coffin-lid can hide

'Tis they who are in their own chambers haunted

By thoughts that like unbidden guests intrude,
And sit down, uninvited and unwanted,
And make a nightmare of the solitude.

HALF FLEDGED

I feel the stirrings in me of great things.
New half-fledged thoughts rise up and beat their wings,
And tremble on the margin of their nest,
Then flutter back, and hide within my breast.

Beholding space, they doubt their untried strength.
Beholding men, they fear them. But at length
Grown all too great and active for the heart
That broods them with such tender mother art,
Forgetting fear, and men, and all, that hour,
Save the impelling consciousness of power
That stirs within them, they shall soar away
Up to the very portals of the Day.

Oh, what exultant rapture thrills me through
When I contemplate all those thoughts may do;
Like snow-white eagles penetrating space,
They may explore full many an unknown place,
And build their nests on mountain heights unseen,
Whereon doth lie that dreamed-of rest serene.

Stay thou a little longer in my breast,
Till my fond heart shall push thee from the nest,
Anxious to see thee soar to heights divine
Oh, beautiful but half-fledged thoughts of mine.

LOVE'S SLEEP
(Vers de Société.)

We'll cover Love with roses,
And sweet sleep he shall take.
None but a fool supposes
Love always keeps awake.
I've known loves without number.
True loves were they, and tried;
And just for want of slumber
They pined away and died.

Our love was bright and cheerful
A little while agone;

Now he is pale and tearful,
And yes, I've seen him yawn.
So tired is he of kisses
That he can only weep;
The one dear thing he misses
And longs for now is sleep.

We could not let him leave us
One time, he was so dear,
But now it would not grieve us
If he slept half a year.
For he has had his season,
Like the lily and the rose,
And it but stands to reason
That he should want repose.

We prized the smiling Cupid
Who made our days so bright;
But he has grown so stupid
We gladly say good-night.
And if he wakens tender
And fond, and fair as when
He filled our lives with splendor,
We'll take him back again.

And should he never waken,
As that perchance may be,
We will not weep forsaken,
But sing, "Love, tra-la-lee!"

TRUE CULTURE

The highest culture is to speak no ill;
The best reformer is the man whose eyes
Are quick to see all beauty and all worth;
And by his own discreet, well-ordered life,
Alone reproves the erring.
When they gaze
Turns it on thine own soul, be most severe.
But when it falls upon a fellow-man
Let kindliness control it; and refrain
From that belittling censure that springs forth
From common lips like weeds from marshy soil.

THE VOLUPTUARY

Oh, I am sick of love reciprocated,

Of hopes fulfilled, ambitions gratified.
Life holds no thing to be anticipated,
And I am sad from being satisfied.

The eager joy felt climbing up the mountain
Has left me now the highest point is gained.
The crystal spray that fell from Fame's fair fountain
Was sweeter than the waters were when drained.

The gilded apple which the world calls pleasure,
And which I purchased with my youth and strength,
Pleased me a moment. But the empty treasure
Lost all its lustre, and grew dim at length.

And love, all glowing with a golden glory,
Delighted me a season with its tale.
It pleased the longest, but at last the story
So oft repeated, to my heart grew stale.

I lived for self, and all I asked was given,
I have had all, and now am sick of bliss,
No other punishment designed by Heaven
Could strike me half so forcibly as this.

I feel no sense of aught but enervation
In all the joys my selfish aims have brought,
And know no wish but for annihilation,
Since that would give me freedom from the thought.

Oh, blest is he who has some aim defeated;
Some mighty loss to balance all his gain.
For him there is a hope not yet completed;
For him hath life yet draughts of joy and pain.

But cursed is he who has no balked ambition,
No hopeless hope, no loss beyond repair,
But sick and sated with complete fruition,
Keeps not the pleasure even of despair.

THE YEAR
What can be said in New Year rhymes,
That's not been said a thousand times?

The new years come, the old years go,
We know we dream, we dream we know.

We rise up laughing with the light,
We lie down weeping with the night.

We hug the world until it stings,
We curse it then and sigh for wings.

We live, we love, we woo, we wed,
We wreathe our brides, we sheet our dead.

We laugh, we weep, we hope, we fear,
And that's the burden of the year.

THE UNATTAINED

A vision beauteous as the morn,
With heavenly eyes and tresses streaming,
Slow glided o'er a field late shorn
Where walked a poet idly dreaming.
He saw her, and joy lit his face,
"Oh, vanish not at human speaking,"
He cried, "thou form of magic grace,
Thou art the poem I am seeking.

"I've sought thee long! I claim thee now
My thought embodied, living, real."
She shook the tresses from her brow.
"Nay, nay!" she said, "I am ideal.
I am the phantom of desire
The spirit of all great endeavor,
I am the voice that says, 'Come higher,'
That calls men up and up forever.

"'Tis not alone thy thought supreme
That here upon thy path has risen;
I am the artist's highest dream,
The ray of light he cannot prison.
I am the sweet ecstatic note
Than all glad music gladder, clearer,
That trembles in the singer's throat,
And dies without a human hearer.

"I am the greater, better yield,
That leads and cheers thy farmer neighbor,
For me he bravely tills the field
And whistles gayly at his labor.
Not thou alone, O poet soul,
Dost seek me through an endless morrow,

But to the toiling, hoping whole
I am at once the hope and sorrow.

The spirit of the unattained,
I am to those who seek to name me,
A good desired but never gained.
All shall pursue, but none shall claim me."

IN THE CROWD

How happy they are, in all seeming,
How gay, or how smilingly proud,
How brightly their faces are beaming,
These people who make up the crowd.
How they bow, how they bend, how they flutter,
How they look at each other and smile,
How they glow, and what bon mots they utter!
But a strange thought has found me the while!

It is odd, but I stand here and fancy
These people who now play a part,
All forced by some strange necromancy
To speak, and to act, from the heart.
What a hush would come over the laughter!
What a silence would fall on the mirth!
And then what a wail would sweep after,
As the night-wind sweeps over the earth.

If the secrets held under and hidden
In the intricate hearts of the crowd,
Were suddenly called to, and bidden
To rise up and cry out aloud,
How strange one would look to another!
Old friends of long standing and years
Own brothers would not know each other,
Robed new in their sorrows and fears.

From broadcloth, and velvet, and laces,
Would echo the groans of despair,
And there would be blanching of faces
And wringing of hands and of hair.
That man with his record of honor,
That lady down there with the rose,
That girl with Spring's freshness upon her,
Who knoweth the secrets of those?

Smile on, O ye maskers, smile sweetly!

Step lightly, bow low and laugh loud!
Though the world is deceived and completely,
I know ye, O sad-hearted crowd!
I watch you with infinite pity:
But play on, play ever your part,
Be gleeful, be joyful, be witty!
'Tis better than showing the heart.

LIFE AND I

Life and I are lovers, straying
Arm in arm along:
Often like two children Maying,
Full of mirth and song.

Life plucks all the blooming hours
Growing by the way;
Binds them on my brow like flowers;
Calls me Queen of May.

Then again, in rainy weather,
We sit vis-a-vis,
Planning work we'll do together
In the years to be.

Sometimes Life denies me blisses,
And I frown or pout;
But we make it up with kisses
Ere the day is out.

Woman-like, I sometimes grieve him,
Try his trust and faith,
Saying I shall one day leave him
For his rival Death.

Then he always grows more zealous,
Tender, and more true;
Loves the more for being jealous,
As all lovers do.

Though I swear by stars above him,
And by worlds beyond,
That I love him, love him, love him;
Though my heart is fond;

Though he gives me, doth my lover,
Kisses with each breath

I shall one day throw him over,
And plight troth with Death.

GUERDON

Upon the white cheek of the Cherub Year
I saw a tear.
Alas! I murmured, that the Year should borrow
So soon a sorrow.
Just then the sunlight fell with sudden flame:
The tear became
A wond'rous diamond sparkling in the light
A beauteous sight.

Upon my soul there fell such woeful loss,
I said, "The Cross
Is grievous for a life as young as mine."
Just then, like wine,
God's sunlight shone from His high Heavens down;
And lo! a crown
Gleamed in the place of what I thought a burden
My sorrow's guerdon.

SNOWED UNDER

Of a thousand things that the Year snowed under
The busy Old Year who has gone away
How many will rise in the Spring, I wonder,
Brought to life by the sun of May?
Will the rose-tree branches, so wholly hidden
That never a rose-tree seems to be,
At the sweet Spring's call come forth unbidden,
And bud in beauty, and bloom for me?

Will the fair, green Earth, whose throbbing bosom
Is hid like a maid's in her gown at night,
Wake out of her sleep, and with blade and blossom
Gem her garments to please my sight?
Over the knoll in the valley yonder
The loveliest buttercups bloomed and grew;
When the snow has gone that drifted them under,
Will they shoot up sunward, and bloom anew?

When wild winds blew, and a sleet-storm pelted,
I lost a jewel of priceless worth;
If I walk that way when snows have melted,
Will the gem gleam up from the bare, brown Earth?

I laid a love that was dead or dying,
For the year to bury and hide from sight;
But out of a trance will it waken, crying,
And push to my heart, like a leaf to the light?

Under the snow lie things so cherished
Hopes, ambitions, and dreams of men
Faces that vanished, and trusts that perished,
Never to sparkle and glow again.
The Old Year greedily grasped his plunder,
And covered it over and hurried away:
Of the thousand things that he did, I wonder
How many will rise at the call of May?
O wise Young Year, with your hands held under
Your mantle of ermine, tell me, pray!

PLATONIC
I knew it the first of the Summer
I knew it the same at the end
That you and your love were plighted,
But couldn't you be my friend?
Couldn't we sit in the twilight,
Couldn't we walk on the shore,
With only a pleasant friendship
To bind us, and nothing more?

There was never a word of nonsense
Spoken between us two,
Though we lingered oft in the garden
Till the roses were wet with dew.
We touched on a thousand subjects
The moon and the stars above;
But our talk was tinctured with science,
With never a hint of love.

"A wholly platonic friendship,"
You said I had proved to you,
"Could bind a man and a woman
The whole long season through,
With never a thought of folly,
Though both are in their youth."
What would you have said, my lady,
If you had known the truth?

Had I done what my mad heart prompted
Gone down on my knees to you,

And told you my passionate story
There in the dusk and dew;
My burning, burdensome story,
Hidden and hushed so long,
My story of hopeless loving
Say, would you have thought it wrong?

But I fought with my heart and conquered:
I hid my wound from sight;
You were going away in the morning
And I said a calm good-night.
But now, when I sit in the twilight
Or when I walk by the sea,
That friendship quite "platonic"
Comes surging over me.
And a passionate longing fills me
For the roses, the dusk and the dew,
For the beautiful Summer vanished
For the moonlit talks and you.

WHAT WE NEEDED

What does our country need? Not armies standing
With sabres gleaming ready for the fight.
Not increased navies, skillful and commanding,
To bound the waters with an iron might.
Not haughty men with glutted purses trying
To purchase souls, and keep the power of place.
Not jeweled dolls with one another vieing
For palms of beauty, elegance and grace.

But we want women, strong of soul, yet lowly,
With that rare meekness, born of gentleness,
Women whose lives are pure and clean and holy,
The women whom all little children bless.
Brave, earnest women, helpful to each other,
With finest scorn for all things low and mean.
Women who hold the names of wife and mother,
Far nobler than the title of a Queen.

O these are they who mold the men of story,
These mothers, ofttimes shorn of grace and youth,
Who, worn and weary, ask no greater glory
Than making some young soul the home of truth,
Who sow in hearts all fallow for the sowing
The seeds of virtue and of scorn for sin,
And, patient, watch the beauteous harvest growing

And weed out tares which crafty hands cast in.

Women who do not hold the gift of beauty
As some rare treasure to be bought and sold,
But guard it as a precious aid to duty
The outer framing of the inner gold;
Women who, low above their cradles bending,
Let flattery's voice go by, and give no heed,
While their pure prayers like incense are ascending:
These are our country's pride, our country's need.

"LEUDEMANN'S-ON-THE-RIVER."
Toward even when the day leans down
To kiss the upturned face of night,
Out just beyond the loud-voiced town
I know a spot of calm delight.
Like crimson arrows from a quiver
The red rays pierce the waters flowing
While we go dreaming, singing, rowing
To Leudemann's-on-the-River.

The hills, like some glad mocking-bird,
Send back our laughter and our singing,
While faint and yet more faint is heard
The steeple bells all sweetly ringing.
Some message did the winds deliver
To each glad heart that August night,
All heard, but all heard not aright;
By Leudemann's-on-the-River.

Night falls as in some foreign clime,
Between the hills that slope and rise.
So dusk the shades at landing time,
We could not see each other's eyes.
We only saw the moonbeams quiver
Far down upon the stream! that night
The new moon gave but little light
By Leudemann's-on-the-River.

How dusky were those paths that led
Up from the river to the hall.
The tall trees branching overhead
Invite the early shades that fall.
In all the glad blithe world, oh, never
Were hearts more free from care than when
We wandered through those walks, we ten,

By Leudemann's-on-the-River.

So soon, so soon, the changes came.
This August day we two alone,
On that same river, not the same,
Dream of a night forever flown.
Strange distances have come to sever
The hearts that gayly beat in pleasure,
Long miles we cannot cross or measure
From Leudemann's-on-the-River.

We'll pluck two leaves, dear friend, to-day.
The green, the russet! seems it strange
So soon, so soon, the leaves can change!
Ah, me! so runs all life away.
This night wind chills me, and I shiver;
The Summer time is almost past.
One more good-bye, perhaps the last
To Leudemann's-on-the-River.

IN THE LONG RUN

In the long run fame finds the deserving man.
The lucky wight may prosper for a day,
But in good time true merit leads the van,
And vain pretense, unnoticed, goes its way.
There is no Chance, no Destiny, no Fate,
But Fortune smiles on those who work and wait,
In the long run.

In the long run all goodly sorrow pays,
There is no better thing than righteous pain,
The sleepless nights, the awful thorn-crowned days,
Bring sure reward to tortured soul and brain.
Unmeaning joys enervate in the end.
But sorrow yields a glorious dividend
In the long run.

In the long run all hidden things are known,
The eye of truth will penetrate the night,
And good or ill, thy secret shall be known,
However well 'tis guarded from the light.
All the unspoken motives of the breast
Are fathomed by the years and stand confest
In the long run.

In the long run all love is paid by love,

Though undervalued by the hosts of earth;
The great eternal Government above
Keeps strict account and will redeem its worth.
Give thy love freely; do not count the cost;
So beautiful a thing was never lost
In the long run.

PLEA TO SCIENCE
O Science reaching backward through the distance,
Most earnest child of God,
Exposing all the secrets of existence,
With thy divining rod,
I bid thee speed up to the heights supernal,
Clear thinker, ne'er sufficed;
Go seek and bind the laws and truths eternal,
But leave me Christ.

Upon the vanity of pious sages
Let in the light of day.
Break down the superstitions of all ages
Thrust bigotry away;
Stride on, and bid all stubborn foes defiance
Let Truth and Reason reign.
But I beseech thee, O Immortal Science,
Let Christ remain.

What canst thou give to help me bear my crosses,
In place of Him, my Lord?
And what to recompense for all my losses,
And bring me sweet reward?
Thou couldst not with thy clear, cold eyes of reason,
Thou couldst not comfort me
Like one who passed through that tear-blotted season,
In sad Gethsemane!

Through all the weary, wearing hour of sorrow,
What word that thou hast said,
Would make me strong to wait for some to-morrow
When I should find my dead?
When I am weak, and desolate, and lonely
And prone to follow wrong?
Not thou, O Science, Christ, my Savior, only
Can make me strong.

Thou are so cold, so lofty and so distant,
Though great my need might be,

No prayer, however constant and persistent,
Could bring thee down to me.
Christ stands so near, to help me through each hour,
To guide me day by day.
O Science, sweeping all before thy power
Leave Christ, I pray!

LOVE'S BURIAL

Let us clear a little space,
And make Love a burial place.

He is dead, dear, as you see,
And he wearies you and me,

Growing heavier, day by day,
Let us bury him, I say.

Wings of dead white butterflies,
These shall shroud him, as he lies

In his casket rich and rare,
Made of finest maiden-hair.

With the pollen of the rose
Let us his white eye-lids close.

Put the rose thorn in his hand,
Shorn of leaves you understand.

Let some holy water fall
On his dead face, tears of gall

As we kneel by him and say,
"Dreams to dreams," and turn away.

Those grave diggers, Doubt, Distrust,
They will lower him to the dust.

Let us part here with a kiss,
You go that way, I go this.

Since we buried Love to-day
We will walk a separate way.

LITTLE BLUE HOOD

Every morning and every night
There passes our window near the street,
A little girl with an eye so bright,
And a cheek so round and a lip so sweet;
The daintiest, jauntiest little miss
That ever any one longed to kiss.

She is neat as wax, and fresh to view,
And her look is wholesome and clean, and good.
Whatever her gown, her hood is blue,
And so we call her our "Little Blue Hood,"
For we know not the name of the dear little lass,
But we call to each other to see her pass.

"Little Blue Hood is coming now!"
And we watch from the window while she goes by,
She has such a bonny, smooth, white brow,
And a fearless look in her long-lashed eye;
And a certain dignity wedded to grace,
Seems to envelop her form and face.

Every morning, in sun or rain,
She walks by the window with sweet, grave air,
And never guesses behind the pane
We two are watching and thinking her fair;
Lovingly watching her down the street,
Dear little Blue Hood, bright and sweet.

Somebody ties that hood of blue
Under the face so fair to see,
Somebody loves her, beside we two,
Somebody kisses her, why can't we?
Dear Little Blue Hood fresh and fair,
Are you glad we love you, or don't you care?

NO SPRING

Up from the South come the birds that were banished,
Frightened away by the presence of frost.
Back to the vale comes the verdure that vanished,
Back to the forest the leaves that were lost.
Over the hillside the carpet of splendor,
Folded through Winter, Spring spreads down again;
Along the horizon, the tints that were tender,
Lost hues of Summer time, burn bright as then.

Only the mountains' high summits are hoary,

To the ice-fettered river the sun gives a key.
Once more the gleaming shore lists to the story
Told by an amorous Summer-kissed sea.
All things revive that in Winter time perished,
The rose buds again in the light o' the sun,
All that was beautiful, all that was cherished,
Sweet things and dear things and all things save one.

Late, when the year and the roses were lying
Low with the ruins of Summer and bloom,
Down in the dust fell a love that was dying,
And the snow piled above it, and made it a tomb.
Lo! now! the roses are budded for blossom
Lo! now! the Summer is risen again.
Why dost thou bud not, O Love of my bosom?
Why dost thou rise not, and thrill me as then?

Life without love, is a year without Summer,
Heart without love, is a wood without song.
Rise then, revive then, thou indolent comer,
Why dost thou lie in the dark earth so long?
Rise! ah, thou canst not! the rose-tree that sheddest
Its beautiful leaves, in the Spring time may bloom,
But of cold things the coldest, of dead things the deadest,
Love buried once, rises not from the tomb.
Green things may grow on the hillside and heather,
Birds seek the forest and build there and sing.
All things revive in the beautiful weather,
But unto a dead love there cometh no Spring.

LIPPO

Now we must part, my Lippo. Even so,
I grieve to see thy sudden pained surprise;
Gaze not on me with such accusing eyes
'T was thine own hand which dealt dear Love's death-blow.

I loved thee fondly yesterday. Till then
Thy heart was like a covered golden cup
Always above my eager lip held up.
I fancied thou wert not as other men.

I knew that heart was filled with Love's sweet wine,
Pressed wholly for my drinking. And my lip
Grew parched with thirsting for one nectared sip
Of what, denied me, seemed a draught divine.

Last evening, in the gloaming, that cup spilled
Its precious contents. Even to the lees
Were offered to me, saying, "Drink of these!"
And when I saw it empty, Love was killed.

No word was left unsaid, no act undone,
To prove to me thou wert my abject slave.
Ah, Love! hadst thou been wise enough to save
One little drop of that sweet wine but one

I still had loved thee, longing for it then.
But even the cup is mine. I look within,
And find it holds not one last drop to win,
And cast it down. Thou art as other men.

MIDSUMMER

After the May time, and after the June time
Rare with blossoms and perfumes sweet,
Cometh the round world's royal noon time,
The red midsummer of blazing heat.
When the sun, like an eye that never closes,
Bends on the earth its fervid gaze,
And the winds are still, and the crimson roses
Droop and wither and die in its rays.

Unto my heart has come that season,
O my lady, my worshiped one,
When over the stars of Pride and Reason
Sails Love's cloudless, noonday sun.
Like a great red ball in my bosom burning
With fires that nothing can quench or tame.
It glows till my heart itself seems turning
Into a liquid lake of flame.

The hopes half shy, and the sighs all tender,
The dreams and fears of an earlier day,
Under the noontide's royal splendor,
Droop like roses and wither away.
From the hills of doubt no winds are blowing,
From the isle of pain no breeze is sent.
Only the sun in a white heat glowing
Over an ocean of great content.

Sink, O my soul, in this golden glory,
Die, O my heart, in thy rapture-swoon,
For the Autumn must come with its mournful story,

And Love's midsummer will fade too soon.

A REMINISCENCE
I saw the wild honey-bee kissing a rose
A wee one, that grows
Down low on the bush, where her sisters above
Cannot see all that's done
As the moments roll on.
Nor hear all the whispers and murmurs of love.

They flaunt out their beautiful leaves in the sun,
And they flirt, every one,
With the wild bees who pass, and the gay butterflies.
And that wee thing in pink
Why, they never once think
That she's won a lover right under their eyes.

It reminded me, Kate, of a time, you know when!
You were so petite then,
Your dresses were short, and your feet were so small.
Your sisters, Maud-Belle
And Madeline, well,
They both set their caps for me, after that ball.

How the blue eyes and black eyes smiled up in my face!
'T was a neck-and-neck race,
Till that day when you opened the door in the hall,
And looked up and looked down,
With your sweet eyes of brown,
And you seemed so tiny, and I felt so tall.

Your sisters had sent you to keep me, my dear,
Till they should appear.
Then you were dismissed like a child in disgrace.
How meekly you went!
But your brown eyes, they sent
A thrill to my heart, and a flush to my face.

We always were meeting some way after that.
You hung up my hat,
And got it again, when I finished my call.
Sixteen, and so sweet!
Oh, those cute little feet!
Shall I ever forget how they tripped down the hall?

Shall I ever forget the first kiss by the door,

Or the vows murmured o'er,
Or the rage and surprise of Maud-Belle? Well-a-day,
How swiftly time flows,
And who would suppose
That a bee could have carried me so far away.

RESPITE

The mighty conflict, which we call existence,
Doth wear upon the body and the soul.
Our vital forces wasted in resistance,
So much there is to conquer and control.

The rock which meets the billows with defiance.
Undaunted and unshaken day by day,
In spite of its unyielding self-reliance,
Is by the warfare surely worn away.

And there are depths and heights of strong emotions
That surge at times within the human breast,
More fierce than all the tides of all the oceans
Which sweep on ever in divine unrest.

I sometimes think the rock worn with adventures,
And sad with thoughts of conflicts yet to be,
Must envy the frail reed which no one censures,
When overcome 'tis swallowed by the sea.

This life is all resistance and repression,
Dear God, if in that other world unseen,
Not rest, we find, but new life and progression,
Grant us a respite in the grave between.

A GIRL'S FAITH

Across the miles that stretch between,
Through days of gloom or glad sunlight,
There shines a face I have not seen
Which yet doth make my world more bright.

He may be near, he may be far,
Or near or far I cannot see,
But faithful as the morning star
He yet shall rise and come to me.

What though fate leads us separate ways,
The world is round, and time is fleet.

A journey of a few brief days,
And face to face we two shall meet.

Shall meet beneath God's arching skies,
While suns shall blaze, or stars shall gleam,
And looking in each other's eyes
Shall hold the past but as a dream.

But round and perfect and complete,
Life like a star shall climb the height,
As we two press with willing feet
Together toward the Infinite.

And still behind the space between,
As back of dawns the sunbeams play,
There shines the face I have not seen,
Whose smile shall wake my world to Day.

TWO

One leaned on velvet cushions like a queen
To see him pass, the hero of an hour,
Whom men called great. She bowed with languid mien,
And smiled, and blushed, and knew her beauty's power.

One trailed her tinseled garments through the street,
And thrust aside the crowd, and found a place
So near, the blooded courser's praning feet
Cast sparks of fire upon her painted face.

One took the hot-house blossoms from her breast,
And tossed them down, as he went riding by.
And blushed rose-red to see them fondly pressed
To bearded lips, while eye spoke unto eye.

One, bold and hardened with her sinful life,
Yet shrank and shivered painfully, because
His cruel glance cut keener than a knife,
The glance of him who made her what she was.

One was observed, and lifted up to fame,
Because the hero smiled upon her! while
One who was shunned and hated, found her shame
In basking in the death-light of his smile.

SLIPPING AWAY

Slipping away, slipping away!
Out of our brief year slips the May;
And Winter lingers, and Summer flies;
And Sorrow abideth, and Pleasure dies;
And the days are short, and the nights are long;
And little is right, and much is wrong.

Slipping away is the Summer time;
It has lost its rhythm and lilting rhyme
For the grace goes out of the day so soon,
And the tired headaches in the glare of noon,
And the way seems long to the hills that lie
Under the calm of the western sky.

Slipping away are the friends whose worth
Lent a glow to the sad old earth:
One by one they slip from our sight;
One by one their graves gleam white;
Or we count them lost by the crueler death
Of a trust betrayed, or a murdered faith.

Slipping away are the hopes that made
Bliss out of sorrow, and sun out of shade.
Slipping away is our hold on life.
And out of the struggle and wearing strife,
From joys that diminish, and woes that increase,
We are slipping away to the shores of Peace.

IS IT DONE?
It is done! in the fire's fitful flashes,
The last line has withered and curled.
In a tiny white heap of dead ashes
Lie buried the hopes of your world.
There were mad foolish vows in each letter,
It is well they have shriveled and burned,
And the ring! oh, the ring was a fetter,
It was better removed and returned.

But ah, is it done? in the embers
Where letters and tokens were cast,
Have you burned up the heart that remembers,
And treasures its beautiful past?
Do you think in this swift reckless fashion
To ruthlessly burn and destroy
The months that were freighted with passion,
The dreams that were drunken with joy?

Can you burn up the rapture of kisses
That flashed from the lips to the soul?
Or the heart that grows sick for lost blisses
In spite of its strength of control?
Have you burned up the touch of warm fingers
That thrilled through each pulse and each vein,
Or the sound of a voice that still lingers
And hurts with a haunting refrain?

Is it done? is the life drama ended?
You have put all the lights out, and yet,
Though the curtain, rung down, has descended,
Can the actors go home and forget?
Ah, no! they will turn in their sleeping
With a strange restless pain in their hearts,
And in darkness, and anguish and weeping,
Will dream they are playing their parts.

A LEAF

Somebody said, in the crowd, last eve,
That you were married, or soon to be.
I have not thought of you, I believe,
Since last we parted. Let me see:
Five long Summers have passed since then
Each has been pleasant in its own way
And you are but one of a dozen men
Who have played the suitor a Summer day.

But, nevertheless, when I heard your name,
Coupled with some one's, not my own,
There burned in my bosom a sudden flame,
That carried me back to the day that is flown.
I was sitting again by the laughing brook,
With you at my feet, and the sky above,
And my heart was fluttering under your look
The unmistakable look of Love.

Again your breath, like a South wind, fanned
My cheek, where the blushes came and went;
And the tender clasp of your strong, warm hand
Sudden thrills through my pulses sent.
Again you were mine by Love's own right
Mine forever by Love's decree:
So for a moment it seemed last night,
When somebody mentioned your name to me.

Just for the moment I thought you mine
Loving me, wooing me, as of old.
The tale remembered seemed half divine
Though I held it lightly enough when told.
The past seemed fairer than when it was near,
As "Blessings brighten when taking flight;"
And just for the moment I held you dear
When somebody mentioned your name last night.

AESTHETIC

In a garb that was guiltless of colors
She stood, with a dull, listless air
A creature of dumps and of dolors,
But most undeniably fair.

The folds of her garment fell round her,
Revealing the curve of each limb;
Well proportioned and graceful I found her,
Although quite alarmingly slim.

From the hem of her robe peeped one sandal
"High art" was she down to her feet;
And though I could not understand all
She said, I could see she was sweet.

Impressed by her limpness and languor,
I proffered a chair near at hand;
She looked back a mild sort of anger
Posed anew, and continued to stand.

Some praises I next tried to mutter
Of the fan that she held to her face;
She said it was "utterly utter,"
And waved it with languishing grace.

I then, in a strain quite poetic,
Begged her gaze on the bow in the sky,
She looked, said its curve was "æsthetic."
But the "tone was too dreadfully high."

Her lovely face, lit by the splendor
That glorified landscape and sea,
Woke thoughts that were daring and tender:
Did her thoughts, too, rest upon me?

"Oh, tell me," I cried, growing bolder,
"Have I in your musings a place?"
"Well, yes," she said over her shoulder:
"I was thinking of nothing in space."

POEMS OF THE WEEK

SUNDAY
Lie still and rest, in that serene repose
That on this holy morning comes to those
Who have been burdened with the cares which make
The sad heart weary and the tired head ache.
Lie still and rest
God's day of all is best.

MONDAY
Awake! arise! Cast off thy drowsy dreams!
Red in the East, behold the Morning gleams.
"As Monday goes, so goes the week," dames say.
Refreshed, renewed, use well the initial day.
And see! thy neighbor
Already seeks his labor.

TUESDAY
Another morning's banners are unfurled
Another day looks smiling on the world.
It holds new laurels for thy soul to win:
Mar not its grace by slothfulness or sin,
Nor sad, away,
Send it to yesterday.

WEDNESDAY
Half-way unto the end, the week's high noon.
The morning hours do speed away so soon!
And, when the noon is reached, however bright,
Instinctively we look toward the night.
The glow is lost
Once the meridian crost.

THURSDAY
So well the week has sped, hast thou a friend
Go spend an hour in converse. It will lend
New beauty to thy labors and thy life
To pause a little sometimes in the strife.

Toil soon seems rude
That has no interlude.

FRIDAY
From feasts abstain; be temperate, and pray;
Fast if thou wilt; and yet, throughout the day,
Neglect no labor and no duty shirk:
Not many hours are left thee for thy work
And it were meet
That all should be complete.

SATURDAY
Now with the almost finished task make haste;
So near the night thou hast no time to waste.
Post up accounts, and let thy Soul's eyes look
For flaws and errors in Life's ledger-book.
When labors cease,
How sweet the sense of peace!

GHOSTS
There are ghosts in the room.
As I sit here alone, from the dark corners there
They come out of the gloom,
And they stand at my side and they lean on my chair.

There's the ghost of a Hope
That lighted my days with a fanciful glow,
In her hand is the rope
That strangled her life out. Hope was slain long ago.

But her ghost comes to-night,
With its skeleton face and expressionless eyes,
And it stands in the light,
And mocks me, and jeers me with sobs and with sighs.

There's the ghost of a Joy,
A frail, fragile thing, and I prized it too much,
And the hands that destroy
Clasped it close, and it died at the withering touch.

There's the ghost of a Love,
Born with joy, reared with hope, died in pain and unrest,
But he towers above
All the others, this ghost: yet a ghost at the best.

I am weary, and fain
Would forget all these dead: but the gibbering host
Make my struggle in vain,
In each shadowy corner there lurketh a ghost.

FLEEING AWAY

My thoughts soar not as they ought to soar,
Higher and higher on soul-lent wings;
But ever and often, and more and more
They are dragged down earthward by little things,
By little troubles and little needs,
As a lark might be tangled among the weeds.

My purpose is not what it ought to be,
Steady and fixed, like a star on high,
But more like a fisherman's light at sea;
Hither and thither it seems to fly
Sometimes feeble, and sometimes bright,
Then suddenly lost in the gloom of night.

My life is far from my dream of life
Calmly contented, serenely glad;
But, vexed and worried by daily strife,
It is always troubled, and ofttimes sad
And the heights I had thought I should reach one day
Grow dimmer and dimmer, and farther away.

My heart finds never the longed-for rest;
Its worldly striving, its greed for gold,
Chilled and frightened the calm-eyed guest,
Who sometimes sought me in days of old;
And ever fleeing away from me
Is the higher self that I long to be.

ALL MAD

"He is mad as a hare, poor fellow,
And should be in chains," you say.
I haven't a doubt of your statement,
But who isn't mad, I pray?
Why, the world is a great asylum,
And people are all insane,
Gone daft with pleasure or folly,
Or crazed with passion and pain.

The infant who shrieks at a shadow,
The child with his Santa Claus faith,
The woman who worships Dame Fashion,
Each man with his notions of death,
The miser who hoards up his earnings,
The spendthrift who wastes them too soon,
The scholar grown blind in his delving,
The lover who stares at the moon.

The poet who thinks life a pæan,
The cynic who thinks it a fraud,
The youth who goes seeking for pleasure,
The preacher who dares talk of God,
All priests with their creeds and their croaking,
All doubters who dare to deny,
The gay who find aught to wake laughter,
The sad who find aught worth a sigh,
Whoever is downcast or solemn,
Whoever is gleeful and glad,
Are only the dupes of delusions
We are all of us, all of us mad.

HIDDEN GEMS

We know not what lies in us, till we seek;
Men dive for pearls, they are not found on shore,
The hillsides most unpromising and bleak
Do sometimes hide the ore.

Go, dive in the vast ocean of thy mind,
O man! far down below the noisy waves,
Down in the depths and silence thou mayst find
Rare pearls and coral caves.

Sink thou a shaft into the mine of thought;
Be patient, like the seekers after gold;
Under the rocks and rubbish lieth what
May bring thee wealth untold.

Reflected from the vasty Infinite,
However dulled by earth, each human mind
Holds somewhere gems of beauty and of light
Which, seeking, thou shalt find.

BY-AND-BY

"By-and-by," the maiden sighed "by-and-by

He will claim me for his bride,
Hope is strong and time is fleet;
Youth is fair, and love is sweet,
Clouds will pass that fleck my sky.
He will come back by-and-by, by-and-by."

"By-and-by," the soldier said "by-and-by,
After I have fought and bled,
I shall go home from the wars,
Crowned with glory, seamed with scars.
Joy will flash from some one's eye
When she greets me by-and-by, by-and-by."

"By-and-by," the mother cried "by-and-by,
Strong and sturdy at my side,
Like a staff supporting me,
Will my bonnie baby be.
Break my rest, then, wail and cry
Thou'lt repay me by-and-by, by-and-by."

Fleeting years of time have sped, hurried by
Still the maiden is unwed;
All unknown the soldier lies,
Buried under alien skies;
And the son, with blood-shot eye
Saw his mother starve and die.
God in Heaven! dost Thou on high,
Keep the promised by-and-by, by-and-by?

OVER THE MAY HILL

All through the night time, and all through the day time,
Dreading the morning and dreading the night,
Nearer and nearer we drift to the May time
Season of beauty and season of blight,
Leaves on the linden, and sun on the meadow,
Green in the garden, and bloom everywhere,
Gloom in my heart, and a terrible shadow,
Walks by me, sits by me, stands by my chair.

Oh, but the birds by the brooklet are cheery,
Oh, but the woods show such delicate greens,
Strange how you droop and how soon you are weary
Too well I know what that weariness means.
But how could I know in the crisp winter weather
(Though sometimes I noticed a catch in your breath),
Riding and singing and dancing together,

How could I know you were racing with death?

How could I know when we danced until morning,
And you were the gayest of all the gay crowd
With only that shortness of breath for a warning,
How could I know that you danced for a shroud?
Whirling and whirling through moonlight and starlight,
Rocking as lightly as boats on the wave,
Down in your eyes shone a deep light, a far light,
How could I know 'twas the light to your grave?

Day by day, day by day, nearing and nearing,
Hid under greenness, and beauty and bloom,
Cometh the shape and the shadow I'm fearing,
"Over the May hill" is waiting your tomb.
The season of mirth and of music is over
I have danced my last dance, I have sung my last song,
Under the violets, under the clover,
My heart and my love will be lying ere long.

A SONG
Is anyone sad in the world, I wonder?
Does anyone weep on a day like this,
With the sun above, and the green earth under?
Why, what is life but a dream of bliss?

With the sun, and the skies, and the birds above me,
Birds that sing as they wheel and fly
With the winds to follow and say they love me
Who could be lonely? O ho, not I!

Somebody said, in the street this morning,
As I opened my window to let in the light,
That the darkest day of the world was dawning;
But I looked, and the East was a gorgeous sight.

One who claims that he knows about it
Tells me the Earth is a vale of sin;
But I and the bees and the birds, we doubt it,
And think it a world worth living in.

Someone says that hearts are fickle,
That love is sorrow, that life is care,
And the reaper Death, with his shining sickle,
Gathers whatever is bright and fair.

I told the thrush, and we laughed together,
Laughed till the woods were all a-ring:
And he said to me, as he plumed each feather,
"Well, people must croak, if they cannot sing."

Up he flew, but his song, remaining,
Rang like a bell in my heart all day,
And silenced the voices of weak complaining,
That pipe like insects along the way.

O world of light, and O world of beauty!
Where are there pleasures so sweet as thine?
Yes, life is love, and love is duty;
And what heart sorrows? O no, not mine!

FOES

Thank Fate for foes! I hold mine dear
As valued friends. He cannot know
The zest of life who runneth here
His earthly race without a foe.

I saw a prize. "Run," cried my friend;
"'Tis thine to claim without a doubt."
But ere I half-way reached the end,
I felt my strength was giving out.

My foe looked on the while I ran;
A scornful triumph lit his eyes.
With that perverseness born in man,
I nerved myself, and won the prize.

All blinded by the crimson glow
Of sin's disguise, I tempted Fate.
"I knew thy weakness!" sneered my foe,
I saved myself, and balked his hate.

For half my blessings, half my gain,
I needs must thank my trusty foe;
Despite his envy and disdain,
He serves me well where'er I go.

So may I keep him to the end,
Nor may his enmity abate:
More faithful than the fondest friend,
He guards me ever with his hate.

FRIENDSHIP

Dear friend, I pray thee, if thou wouldst be proving
Thy strong regard for me,
Make me no vows. Lip-service is not loving;
Let thy faith speak for thee.

Swear not to me that nothing can divide us
So little such oaths mean.
But when distrust and envy creep beside us
Let them not come between.

Say not to me the depths of thy devotion
Are deeper than the sea;
But watch, lest doubt or some unkind emotion
Embitter them for me.

Vow not to love me ever and forever,
Words are such idle things;
But when we differ in opinions, never
Hurt me by little stings.

I'm sick of words: they are so lightly spoken,
And spoken, are but air.
I'd rather feel thy trust in me unbroken
Than list thy words so fair.

If all the little proofs of trust are heeded,
If thou art always kind,
No sacrifice, no promise will be needed
To satisfy my mind.

Ella Wheeler Wilcox – A Short Biography

Ella Wheeler was born on 5th November, 1850, on a farm in the village of Johnstown, Rock County, Wisconsin. Her parents, Marcus H. Wheeler and Sarah Pratt Wheeler, already had three children. A year earlier the family had moved from Vermont after Marcus's attempts at show business failed and becoming a farmer was his response. With Ella's birth they moved again. This time further north to Madison.

Ella was a gifted child, writing poetry and novels from an early age. The family was poor but her parents believed in education, and whilst little could be afforded they helped as best they could most usefully with grammar, spelling and vocabulary. Her initial education was at the local district school in the village of Windsor, now re-named in her honour as Ella Wheeler Wilcox School.

During her thirteenth year subscriptions the family had been receiving from the New York Mercury, a popular periodical, ceased. This greatly upset her. Life on the farm was lonely and the magazine had been a source of comfort and information about the big world beyond the farm. The family could not afford its own subscription so Ella had to make other plans.

Her writing ambitions were central to this. She wrote two essays but now had to obtain stamps so she could get her submissions in front of editors. She was corresponding with a young girl, Jean, who was in the freshman class at Madison University. Assuring her friend of future payment she enclosed the letter and essays for the New York Mercury.

By 1866, Jean, at Ella's behest, sent a list of all the monthlies and weeklies on the newsstands and Ella was hard at work saving pennies for postage as she began to mail them en masse with her works. Quickly her family lent their support to help out with her endeavours. Ella's mother especially had always thought her daughter would be the one to find the fame, travel and recognition that she had wanted herself and seeing the efforts Ella was putting in she was only to glad to help.

Soon the house the house was filled with ALL the periodicals. Editors would send magazines, books, pictures, bric-a-brac and tableware in response to Ella's requests and works. Being able to earn these items brought her great satisfaction and honed her skills.

She remembers the period in her autobiography:

"The very first verses I sent for publication were unmercifully "guyed" by my beloved "Mercury." The editor urged me to keep to prose and to avoid any further attempts at rhyme. He said that, while this criticism would wound me temporarily, it would eventually confer a favour on me and the world at large.

"My first check came from Frank Leslie's publishing house. I wrote asking for one of his periodicals to be sent to me in return for three little poems I had composed in one day. In reply came a check for ten dollars, saying I must select which one of some thirteen publications they issued at that time.

This bit of crisp paper opened a perfect floodgate of aspiration, inspiration and ambition for me. I had not thought of earning money so soon. I had expected to obtain only books, magazines and articles of use and beauty from the editor's prize-lists; and I had not supposed verses to be saleable. I wrote them because they came to me, but I expected to be a novelist like Mrs. Southworth and May Agens Fleming in time - that was the goal of my dreams. The check from Leslie was a revelation. I walked, talked, thought and dreamed in verse after that. A day which passed without a poem from my pen I considered lost and misused. Two each day was my idea of industry, and I once achieved eight. They sold, the majority, for three dollars or five dollars each. Sometimes I got ten dollars for a poem, that was always an event. Short love-stories, over which I laboured painfully, as story writing was an acquired habit, also added to my income, bringing me ten or fifteen dollars, and once in a while larger sums, from "Peterson's," "Demorest's," "Harper's Bazaar" and the "Chimney Corner."

Ella was beginning to understand the route to success and had the work ethic and creativity to turn it to her advantage. Ella would write her daily quota of poems and other works and then send them out to editors in the hope of getting them published.

It was also about this time that she also left the Country school. Her record in grammar, spelling, reading had of course been excellent but she had a horror of mathematics preferring to spend as much time as possible in the world of her imagination. Ella's talent and determination was such that by now, after she graduated from High School she was already well known in her state as a young writer.

In this she was encouraged by her mother, who despised her own life and felt herself and her family superior to all her neighbours and was forever impressing on the young teenager that her life would blossom and she would achieve success as a writer.

In 1867 her parents sent her to Madison where she was a junior in the Female College, a part of the University of Wisconsin. Ella wanted to spend all of her time writing and begged to come home. She didn't feel the need for further education and was painfully aware of the difference between her homemade clothes and the dresses of city girl. These and other differences caused her to feel left out and not part of the group. After many requests her parents relented and she was allowed home to continue her writing.

In 1870 she was offered employment at $45 a month to edit the literary department of a publication by the magazine's Milwaukee Editor. She accepted, but the hours and work were not to her liking and after three months the magazine folded and her single experience of working in an office was over. Now she was to be a full time author.

In 1872 she published her first book. It was an unusual step as it was a book of poems entitled 'Drops Of Water: Poems' that were solely about abstinence. Published by the National Temperance society it reflected her views on the evils of alcohol and earned her a $50 fee.

She published further books over the next decade but it wasn't until 1883 and the rather racy, for those times, publication of Poems of Passion that her success moved suddenly forward. It was an immediate and large scale success selling over 60,000 in two years.

That same year was also noteworthy for she was engaged to be married. Robert Wilcox was one of many suitors to the young Ella. He was a silver salesman from Meriden, Connecticut. Although they only met three times before the wedding it was to be the relationship that defined her life and much of her work. They married the following year in 1884.

Her most famous poem, "Solitude", was first published on 25th February, 1883 in an issue of The New York Sun. The inspiration for the poem came as she was travelling to attend the State Governor's inaugural ball in Madison, Wisconsin. Whilst travelling to the celebration she was sitting next to a young woman, dressed in black, who was in obvious distress. Ella comforted her for the whole journey. Recalling the widow's emotional state Ella wrote:

Laugh, and the world laughs with you;
Weep, and you weep alone.
For the sad old earth must borrow its mirth
But has trouble enough of its own

She sent the poem to the Sun and received $5 for her effort. It was collected in the book Poems of Passion shortly after in May 1883.

The newlyweds lived for a short time in Robert's home town of Meriden, Connecticut, before moving to New York City and then to Granite Bay in the Short Beach area of Branford, Connecticut. They built two homes and several cottages on Long Island Sound where they would hold gatherings of their literary and artistic friends.

On May 27, 1887, Ella gave birth to a son. Tragically he was only to survive for a few short hours.

In the early years of their marriage, they both developed an interest in theosophy, New Thought, and spiritualism. As this developed Robert and

Ella Wheeler Wilcox promised each other that whoever died first would return and attempt to communicate with the other.

Ella had by now published many books of poetry as well as novels and other writings. Her writing life was filled with success on a national scale. Some volumes were collections based on a theme others on a particular time. Some of her war poetry that centred on the Great War in Europe is quite compelling. As she was never considered literary but rather mass market a lot of her work has not received the recognition that other lesser writers have obtained.

In 1916 after thirty years of marriage Robert Wilcox died. Ella was naturally devastated and desperate. Rather than dissipate her grief seemed to grow ever more intense as the days and weeks went by with no message from him. She journeyed to California to see the Rosicrucian astrologer, Max Heindel, seeking help in her sorrow as to why she had no word from Robert. She writes:

"In talking with Max Heindel, the leader of the Rosicrucian Philosophy in California, he made very clear to me the effect of intense grief. Mr. Heindel assured me that I would come in touch with the spirit of my husband when I learned to control my sorrow. I replied that it seemed strange to me that an omnipotent God could not send a flash of his light into a suffering soul to bring its conviction when most needed. Did you ever stand beside a clear pool of water, asked Mr. Heindel, and see the trees and skies repeated therein? And did you ever cast a stone into that pool and see it clouded and turmoiled, so it gave no reflection? Yet the skies and trees were waiting above to be reflected when the waters grew calm. So God and your husband's spirit wait to show themselves to you when the turbulence of sorrow is quieted".

It seemed good advice. She wrote herself a short affirmative prayer to help calm her inner turmoil and would repeat it to herself over and over:

"I am the living witness: The dead live: And they speak through us and to us: And I am the voice that gives this glorious truth to the suffering world: I am ready, God: I am ready, Christ: I am ready, Robert."

She had already written in 1915 a booklet 'What I Know About New Thought which had sold over 50,000 copies. These and other books on New Thought, together with her expanding efforts to educate a wider audience to the powers of positive thinking, were a great comfort to her.

Ella expresses this unique blend of New Thought, Spiritualism and Reincarnation with these powerful words:

"As we think, act, and live here today, we built the structures of our homes in spirit realms after we leave earth, and we build karma for future lives, thousands of years to come, on this earth or other planets. Life will assume new dignity, and labour new interest for us, when we come to the knowledge that death is but a continuation of life and labour, in higher planes".

Ella fell ill in France in early 1919. It was breast cancer. She was taken initially to England and then back to her home. She died of the cancer on October 31, 1919.

Her final words in her autobiography 'The Worlds and I' were:

"From this mighty storehouse (of God, and the hierarchies of Spiritual Beings) we may gather wisdom and knowledge, and receive light and power, as we pass through this preparatory room of earth, which is only one of the innumerable mansions in our Father's house. Think on these things".

A Concise Bibliography

1872 Drops of water, poems.
1873 Shells.
1876 Maurine.
1883 Poems of Passion.
1886 Mal Moule'e, a novel.
1886 Perdita, and other stories.
1888 The Adventures of Miss Volney.
1888 Poems of Pleasure.
1891 A Double Life.
1891 How Salvator Won, and other recitations.
1892 Was it Suicide?
1892 The Beautiful Land of Nod.
1892 An Erring Woman's Love.
1892 Sweet Danger.
1893 The Song of the Sandwich.
1893 Men, Women and Emotions.
1896 An Ambitious Man.
1896 Custer, and other poems.
1897 Three Women.
1897 Roger Merritt's Crime.
1901 Every-day Thoughts in Prose and Verse.
1901 Poems of Power.
1902 The Heart of the New Thought.
1902 Kingdom of Love and How Salvator Won.
1902 The Other Woman's Husband.
1902 Poems of Life.

1904	Around the Year with Ella Wheeler Wilcox.
1904	A Woman of the World.
1905	Mizpah; or, the story of Esther, poetical drama in four acts.
1905	Poems of Love.
1905	Poems of Reflection.
1905	The Story of a literary career.
1906	Poems of Sentiment.
1906	New Thought pastels.
1906	Poems of Peace.
1907	The Kingdom of love, and other poems.
1907	The Love Sonnets of Abelard and Heloise.
1908	New Thought - common sense and what life means to me.
1908	Poems of Cheer.
1908	Selected Poems.
1909	Poems of Progress and New Thought Pastels.
1909	Sailing Sunny Seas.
1910	Diary of a Faithless Husband.
1910	The New Hawaiian Girl; a play.
1910	Poems of Experience.
1910	Yesterdays.
1911	Are you Alive?
1912	Picked Poems.
1912	Gems from Ella Wheeler Wilcox.
1912	The Englishman and other Poems.
1914	Poems of Problems.
1914	The art of Being Alive.
1914	Cameos.
1914	Lest we Forget.
1914	Poems of Ella Wheeler Wilcox.
1915	Poems of Optimism.
1916	World Voices.
1916	More Poems.
1916	Poems of Purpose.
1917	Poetical Works of Ella Wheeler Wilcox.
1918	Sonnets of Sorrow and Triumph.
1918	The Worlds and I.
1919	Poems.
1919	Cinema Poems and others.
1919	Hello Boys!

Published Posthumously

1920	Poems of Affection.
1920	Great Thoughts For Each Day's Life.
1924	Collected Poems of Ella Wheeler Wilcox.
1927	Gems from E.W.Wilcox

www.ingramcontent.com/pod-product-compliance
Lightning Source LLC
Chambersburg PA
CBHW060141050426

42448CB00010B/2232